Oh Sister, My Sister
An An

Diane L. Akins, A

Marie Carpenter, Claudia Chapline, Jane DeJonghe,

Charlene Ellington, Susan Fernie, Carole Fults,

Priscilla Gifford, Ann Griffin, Marietta Harris,

Elena Hoffrichter, Linda Holbrook,

Holly Hunter, Trish Lindsey Jaggers, Trish Lapidus,

Marcella J. Lively, Dakini Lynn Marlow,

Barbara McDaniel, Curtine Metcalf, Cindy Morris,

Jo-Ann Jeannine Kling Murdach, Leslie B. Neustadt,

Laurie Kay Olson, Julie Ann Orecchio, Annette Price,

Christine Price, Terra Rafael, ReneRatchek,

Prema Rose, Bev Simpson, Nancy Schluntz,

Karen Stewart, April Bennett Stone, Bob Surrette,

Lesley Tabor, Barbara Truncellito, Bobbie Vetter,

Jyoti Wind

Edited by Jyoti Wind

Illustrator:
Kathleen Spencer Johns

Starshine Publishing
Boulder, CO

Also by Jyoti Wind:

By Grace's Edge: Poetry, Prose and Prayers
Into the Heart of the Flower: Poetry, Prose and Meditations
Dreaming It Was Real: A Childhood Memoir
Edited: *A Week's Worth of Women*
Edited: *Food and What Feeds Us*
Edited: *Unraveling Mysteries: An Anthology on Women and Aging*
Edited: *The Creative Arc: An Anthology on Writing*
One Small Sip: A Book of Contemplative Poetry

Cover photograph: Jyoti Wind
Cover design: Lanai Bayne
Back cover photograph: Carol Scott Stevens

To order books:
Jyoti Wind
2635 Mapleton Ave. #9
Boulder, CO 80304
www.jyotiwindastrology.com

ii

Dedication to my sister, Kathryn Jean Geiger
Feb. 23, 1948 - Nov. 16, 2014

"I have a feeling of well-being that I never had
when I was there. I feel free."
KJG Nov. 23, 2014

Table of Contents

Introduction

Sisters come in many shapes and sizes. Some are blood-born, others come to us through other families and parts of the world.

The kinship we feel, or feel we should feel, is real and evokes emotions and responses meant to help us grow one way or another.

Sometimes our distance serves the purpose to show us ourselves, into those deeper regions where only we venture.

Other times the bond is so close, so deep, we feel met at a soul level and this reminds us that we are not alone. Carrying on is suddenly easier.

Wherever these souls find us, at home in the family unit, or in a class or even in our neighborhood, they bring us the relationship that opens our lives and moves us along in the direction we have chosen.

From the Beginning

We sat under trees in
Van Cortlandt Park
in the 50s
with horses on the bridle path
and their droppings underfoot.
Neither of us had seen
live horses before.

The tall apartment buildings
of the Bronx enclosed us
like canyons in the west
where I would eventually move.

The seaside beaches held
our summers like book ends
carousels became our delight
with cotton candy in hand.

Her toothy smile and blond curls
were the antithesis of
my bookish seriousness
and we played out those opposites
all our lives.

We had different paths
to walk, different trails
through those initial woods
that would wind back around
years later,

and bring us to a renewal.
I'm glad she was there
a voice in the dark at night
in the bedroom we shared
from the beginning.

Jyoti Wind

Siblings

We were almost her siblings.
She was four when we slipped out-- not yet ready.
Too early to breathe, too soon even to cry.
Quickly, the two of us, here and gone.

She grew up alone, fiercely loved,
Never knowing we had almost been there.
No sharing of bedrooms and angel food cake.
No passing down the dresses that grandma sewed.
No tugging over toys, no scrambling for lap time.
No giggling together under the covers.
No Parcheesi and popcorn.
No smiling family wedding photos.
No nieces or nephews.
She never knew about us.

Much later, she learned of us by chance,
Only a few words from a friend, nothing more.
We remained hidden in our parent's remembering hearts.

Now, years gone by, our sister remains an only, lonely child,
Wishing we had grown and cried and loved together,
Wanting to review her life with someone who had shared all the
years.

Waiting to meet us, at last.

Priscilla Gifford

On A Sister's Birthday

Remember that summer when we were young,
the long brushy slog up the South Fork
of the Cascade River,
Swearing at slide alder,
heavy smell of tangled undergrowth,
insinuating spires of Devil's Club,
yellow-jacket nests in crumbling logs.

Our legs were brown and young,
eager to get above the green,
to test the mountain steps of
Jo-Berg's dark-chunked rocks.

Remember Joe and his martini on the summit?
We looked at each other, lightly scandalized
at the breach of Mountaineering
no-alcohol etiquette.

Remember the tired legs,
picking our way down,
relieved to have summited,

wary, knowing the risk
of weary muscles, misplaced feet.

The sun didn't shine much that day.
A quiet overcast, no dramatic
skies or brilliant peaks.

Just two sisters, sometimes reaching a hand.
No intimations of the years that stood ahead,
the rejections, and reunions,
the traveling toward that other autumn day,
the year your birthday came too late,
And you went on from the summit
Alone.

Lesley Tabor

Big Sister

Suffered the drag of this younger tag-along,
Embarrassed by my over-eager crush
On her oblivious friend
Who thought I liked his younger brother.

She tickled me mercilessly, until I peed my pants,
Locked me in a bathroom until I shaved my legs,
Decided I would look good as a redhead,
And redhead I became for twenty years.

Little sister me, awkward, clumsy, inept
The brunt of teasing by her friends.
Big Sister said "Stop!
No one gets to pick on my sister but me."

Big Sister – the creative one, the pretty one.
At boarding school she led the way,
Watched over me, advocated for me,
Tried to share social skills that came naturally to her.

It all went over my head, cocooned as I was,
Sensing, feeling, no words to describe
The deep and private world that was mine.
Not a good fit in the day to day was I . . . am I.

She witnessed my confusion, betrayed,
The day our mother redecorated my room,
Adding frills and discarding "childish" things.

"Where's my stuff?" Did my feelings matter?
Big Sister understood and came to find me,
Sitting silent, alone, uncomprehending.

▶

We each flowed in and out of the blessing and curse
Of being Favorite Daughter.
Balancing, counterbalancing, she building bridges
When my rebellion sought to destroy them.

We went our separate ways
Into marriage, children, maturity,
Moved to different parts of the country
Busy with our own lives.

She the creative one, the pretty one
Painter, gardener, adventurous,
Adept hostess presenting edible art.

Me the quiet one, awkward still, unsure
Observer, mystic, slow to learn
How to express the world within.

She took the lead when mother's health declined
Receiving list upon list, directives from the matriarch,
Bearing it all with grace.
I just visited.

Children grown, Big Sister and I reconnect.
Finding our sense of who we are
In this world, inside ourselves, together.

Friends now,
She there for me, now I for her,
We each have the other.
And we both write.

Thank you, Big Sister.

Nancy Schluntz

Who's That?

Who is this stranger who comes to visit my house? Why do Mom and Daddy welcome her so happily? What? I have a sister?

Shirley Mary was named for our mother and our two grandmothers. I have no idea where they got my name! When I was born she was already twelve years old. I have a large studio photo of her giving me a bottle of water when I was 5 or 6 months old. She is very young and very pretty. We are both smiling.

That has been pretty much our relationship throughout our lives. We have lived at great physical distances but when we are together we both enjoy the comfort of each other's company. I have asked questions: was I an accident? And she would supply answers when she could. In this case, a definitive NO.

Now we are both older. I was 78 on July 3 and she was 90 last February 15. I flew to Minnesota for her very special day and celebrated with her family: kids, grandkids and great-grand kids. Ironically, she and Cliff, my bother-in-law, are now living in a retirement center in Duluth near the same facility where our father died and where, in another life, I was a nun. Life is truly amazing.

Jo-Ann Jeannine Kling Murdach

Meet on the Mountain

We all need someone to bring out
the greatness within us, someone
to inspire us to remember what it was
like before the rain and to help us
to use the energy from the storm
to progress until we see the light
at the end of the tunnel, someone
to talk to on the way to the summit,
someone to lessen the lonely
and magnify the lovely in the world.

No one knows the spectacular joy
at the top, at the moment of victory,
except the few who have climbed the
hill and cared enough to make the
necessary sacrifices great goals
require.

And those who make the journey
together are forever joined in some
special sameness, like sisters,
but more...
whoever meets on the mountain
will never be satisfied with a lesser
view or lesser friends.

Linda Holbrook

The Nude Rooftop Terrorist of North Street

"Are you kidding me? You've got to be kidding!"

It was my sister's friend, Pat, on the phone, telling me latest exploits of my alcoholic, bi-polar, drug-crazed sister.

Dawn was in Arkansas, staying for a while with my 80 year old mother. Dawn had broken Mother's heart countless times, but being the loving person Mother was, she would always rescue Dawn one more time.

This time Dawn had pissed off everyone in the valley one too many times. She lived in the Huerfano valley in Southern Colorado. It was a hand-to-mouth, subsistence lifestyle, away from mainstream society and its judgments and values. Not the kind of lifestyle I would care for myself, but she was free to play her music, do her art, and drink and party as much as she wanted to. I spent a lot of time being pissed at her excesses, but part of me did envy her that freedom.

Once in while, though, she would get out of control manic and pull some stunt that would get her arrested or hospitalized. She had done a couple of stints at the Pueblo State Hospital, and this time she ended up in the Arkansas State Hospital in Little Rock.

Apparently, she had gotten pissed at something and stomped out of Mother's house, heading down North Street toward the old hospital. Pat was there visiting, and she followed her in her little truck. Dawn ended up at the wound clinic, where my mother had been going for treatment of an open, oozing spot on her ankle.

Pat parked and tried to get Dawn into the truck and get her home. But Dawn just got more and more angry and crazed and Pat couldn't do anything with her. When Dawn was in this kind of state, she was surprisingly physically strong.

Dawn stormed into the wound clinic, yelling and terrorizing the poor women at the front desk. Somehow she got a hold of a couple of computer monitors and threw them on the floor, so the police were called. I guess security chased her out of the building, but she still wouldn't leave. She climbed up on the roof, and proceeded to take off her clothes. So when the police arrived, they found this 5'2" buck naked crazy woman shouting obscenities and threats at them. The policemen called for backup.

They tried several approaches, but Dawn fought them off. They finally had to throw a blanket over her and capture her like a wild animal. I talked to the policeman in charge a couple of days later, and he said that it would certainly go down in the annals of the department as one of their most memorable collars.

That time, Dawn was put in the state hospital in Little Rock, and my Mother got a couple of months of rest. The good people of Fayetteville were once again safe from the nude rooftop terrorist of North Street. And I could only shake my head and wonder what was coming next.

Elena Hoffrichter

It's sad
that it takes
the death of a mother
for two sisters
to come together...

Rene Ratchek

Japanese Doll

Porcelain face,
Silken robes of red embroidered with bright flowers,
High piled lacquered poufs of black hair,
Magical gift from joyous Aunt,
Adored,
Too precious to play with.
She was my sister's, never mine.
Why?
I was the namesake!

Lesley Tabor

Anne

It's over a year, going on two
that you have passed away, still
I think of you, how could I not
you are in each room of my home

gifts given that were treasures to me
the challenge of presenting you, also
shared love of similar passions, tastes
shared adventures as we traveled together
shared stories without the burden of solving
problems, without judgment, without remorse
the telling and not repeating was enough for us

Your picture, a smiling, happy face hangs near me
Your letter written the day before, completes the set
I see it every day, a sister-not by blood but by a life shared

Arlene Sandra Bice

Sisterhood

I am no sister,
but I am a sister's friend;
I understand what
it is to be related;
I know what it is
to be committed to someone,
and I am not concerned
that blood does not flow
between us;
I am also not concerned
with the politics
of relationship,
for we are infinitely
matched up
on an emotional map
we don't need directions
and we know how to find
our way through it
to the very end
of the road.

Linda Holbrook

enveloped
by my soul sister's
soothing ways

Jane DeJonghe

Sisterless Spouse's Sister

My Spouse is an only child, as was I for the first twenty-six months of my life, a head start that lasted until my early teens, when my younger Brother eclipsed me in a number of ways. When I was a dozen or so years old we two boys were both eclipsed in our Mother's heart forever by the arrival, in the usual way, of a Daughter, followed shortly thereafter by the perennial baby of the family, another superfluous Son. This was quite a feat during that age at my Mother's age. No big deal anymore.

In her teen years Spouse made friends with another teenager almost exactly her same age and her eventual best Friend forever. Spouse and Friend lived at home, worked weekdays and danced away the weekends on the north shore of the St. Lawrence Seaway. They dated but nothing stuck, for which I am grateful.

The families were neighbors until Spouse's left the Heights and moved further west, but not so far as to make it impossible to stay close with Friend. Neither had cars but public transportation was convenient, safe and reasonable, as it is to this day. Most times they met at a common locale.

The first threat to their relationship came when Spouse fell for a Cape Codder. She was vacationing here in a cottage colony in Yarmouth owned and operated by my family. We met at the pool. You know how that happens.

Spouse had another few years at home in Friend's orbit as I was out of the picture geographically. I had been involuntarily inducted into our armed services and was dispatched to serve our great nation at the forward edge of the cold war battle area. My tenuous hold on my nascent relationship with my bonnie lassie from north of the border consisted of monthly calls from a pay phone in the post office and occasionally letters. O.K., I wrote every day. It was a combination of young love for a lovely lady and a life-long love of writing.

I am sure my eventual Spouse was tempted with boys next door and others whilst I was away. I never got a "Dear John-Bob" letter. Fortunately Spouse and Friend remained available. How close were they? They were like Sisters.

Friend became the Sister Spouse never had. It wasn't like real Sisters, though. Unlike real siblings there was no downside, no conflict, no dissension. It was all good all the time as it remains to this day, more than half a century later. Hard to believe but true. I kid you not.

I am sure Spouse's Sister-Friend was happy for her when informed that the American soldier boy had asked her to marry him—and that she had said, "Yes!" But you gotta believe it was tinged with pain at the thought of losing Spouse's presence in her life. Surely Sister-Friend realized that we would not settle in Canada, what with America being so nearby and I being a citizen by birth, a birth that came with a long and hard delivery in a blizzard. Thanks Mom and thanks Dad for getting Mom to the hospital with her wearing your hip boots.

Once officially hitched, Spouse joined me in my bivouac overseas and we settled in to see Europe as only residents can. Sister-Friend came and stayed with us when our Daughter was born, born a decent interval after we'd gotten married. Other friends and family were thousands of miles away. Spouse was very happy to have her Sister stay with us in a great number of dimensions, not the least of which was to have someone to speak Canadian English with. Needless to say, I mini-bonded with Sister. She quickly went from Spouse's Sister-Friend to my Friend, to my Sister-Friend.

Good big Brother that I was, I fixed her up with a co-worker at my work, an upstate New Yorker also reluctantly under arms. Spouse stood for her Sister in the little post chapel and followed her into the big city in a snow storm to get officially wed in the town hall as our country of residence required. We walked the newlyweds to the train station the next day as their honeymoon started on a careless Sunday. Do you remember them?

▶

Ah, the military life. I was transferred back to the United States, got out and settled into a civilian job working for the Pentagon. Sister-Friend's Spouse got out, got back in again and spent years overseas in a different land. In the transition he had turned in his muddy boots and put on silver wings. Spouse and Sister stayed in touch but it was tough as Al hadn't invented the Internet yet.

But as lady luck would have it, a few years later Sister-Friend's Spouse was transferred to a stateside post just on the other side of our state's eastern border, less than an hour away from our home--if one is lucky with traffic. He got out and settled into series of government jobs, one of which he holds to this time. Spouse and Sister were together again; not in the same neighborhood, but in neighboring states.

The two girls from the true north's relationship blossomed further, if that was possible. We spent many holidays dining at Sister's table with their children and others who found great hospitality in her home. In recent years the two ladies have carpooled on trips home to see their parents. The girls have also vacationed together sans hubbies by hubbies' druthers. Spouse stood for Sister-Friend's Daughter at her confirmation by the Daughter's request.

Spouse's time with her Sister is the best of times for her and I am sure it is reciprocated. How lucky can two good girls be? We two families are so close that I joked once about a future time, a time I hope is a long way away. These two best friends forever are in a nursing home and are sitting in front of a roaring gas fireplace with machine-made quilts over their laps. One turns to the other and says, "Remember those nice American boys we were married to?"The other nods knowing and then asks, "Which one was mine and which one was yours?"

Bob Surrette

After All

We played and grated on each other,
sisters stacked three to a room in bunks and trundle.
It was a pink room.
Cindy liked pink, so I didn't
until I finally grew up after menopause.
Cindy liked Barbies. I was a tomboy.
We screamed fiercely, hitting each other with hairbrushes,
expressing justified, misdirected anger.
Lori was my pretend baby, eight years younger than me.
As a toddler she'd sit on my lap and fondle my ear lobe.
Michelle was the youngest. I was mad at Mom when she told me
she was pregnant the 6th time - one more kid for me to take care
    of.
I was the oldest, caregiver as well as playmate.
Cooking dinner and watching the kids when Mom was at work.
I imagined I'd already had my allotted children
until I finally grew up when I was pregnant.
Girls, we fought over who would wash dishes, who would wipe
    dishes.
Brothers were exempt. When I left home Dad bought a dishwasher.

Now we circle our separate worlds to support Mom, declining in
    dementia,
following Dad down that rocky road.
Sisters supporting each other as we can-
Cindy, a long-time widow, lost her job of 30 years in her 50's.
Lori questioned her second marriage and knit it back together.
Michelle loves her dog and gambling at the casino like Mom &
    Dad did.
I am the black sheep, far from where I grew up, living a life they
    don't relate to.
We still love each other after all.

Terra Rafael

I couldn't see her face for the blood. It was red and bright and streaming into her eyes and down onto her clothes. She ran screaming to me on the neighborhood street, and I grabbed her hand and ran with her, pulling her behind me. We ran into the apartment to my mother.

She took one look at Kathy and scooping her up, took the elevator up one floor to the resident doctor, Dr. Markman's office. I stayed with my grandparents up the hall for that hour, very scared and worried for my sister.

When I saw her again, she was propped up on pillows in my mother's bed, her six year old head swathed in bandages like a stark white turban. Her blue eyes were watered down from crying, red around the edges, and so light blue they almost seemed like she had cried out some of the color. She'd had eleven stitches in her forehead on the right side.

There was a knock on the door and a small plump woman with dark hair entered, pushing her eight year old son in front of her. His face was solemn with a smirk lurking at the edges. They approached Kathy and my mother as I sat on the far side of the double bed and watched.

Joel was supposed to apologize for pushing my sister into the steel-tipped corner of the drugstore window when he got angry at something that happened. He mumbled something, his mother smiled and they left. I remember seeing the expression of incredulousness cross my mother's face, and which quickly turned to anger. She was furious at their lack of true caring.

Three nights later, as I lay sleeping in my bed in the next room, I was awakened to rushing, and hushed whispers. My father came in to tell me that the stitches had burst in my sister's forehead and they were rushing her to the hospital by taxi. My grandfather would come back and stay with me until they returned.

▶

21

I went back to sleep and the next morning everyone was home exhausted from the middle of the night scare. Kathy was okay now, after the doctor scraped out small metallic particles that had been left in the wound inadvertently. The new sixteen stitches left a long scar and was covered with blonde bangs for all of her childhood.

Jyoti Wind
Reprinted from Dreaming It Was Real: A Childhood Memoir

Andrea

She, my sister Andrea, was twenty-two months and three days older than me, a fact that I was never allowed to forget. She was beautiful, with long auburn sausage curls, green almond shaped eyes, and, oh so good. She was very shy and never did anything wrong, at least in my parents' perception.

I, on the other hand, was into everything. My curls were blond and completely unruly. So was my demeanor. I was boisterous and flamboyant, outgoing and naughty. Or so it was in my parents' perception.

My sister and I were raised by governesses and our grandparents. Our mother and father were away a lot on business or traveling the world. They were in the New York City theater and art scene and were often entertaining famous people. I loved to watch my mother get ready for the plethora of parties.

I knew my sister to be devious and she went out of her way to get me in trouble, not a hard thing to do.

We were at my grandparents' house in Purchase one summer day, when my grandfather was taking photos of us posed on a stone wall that bordered the patio. We were in our white pinafores with bows in our hair, so prim and proper. I must have been about three years old. Just as my grandfather was about to snap the picture, Andrea snuck her hand over and pinched my thigh as hard as she could. I turned and glowered at her as the camera shutter clicked.

There it is for all time, the photo of me, about to cry and angry, and Andrea smiling beatifically as though nothing had happened.

That summarized much of our relationship. She would hole up in her room reading and I would go to great lengths to get her attention. I was, under pain of death, not allowed to put foot into

▶

her room. I would stand at the door and slip my big toe over the threshold, just to get a reaction.

"What good is it to have a sister when she won't play with me?" I bemoaned.

She has never approved of me and my life choices. I went into the theater and then lived around the world. She became an architect and lived around the world.

Our lives on the earth together have become distantly friendly and polite. She sends me news of her family and I do the same. We no longer fight like "cats and dogs". We even had fun together when I visited her at her home in France. I hope that even after seventy-some years of relative estrangement we can, now, really relate to each other as sisters. In spite of all the distance, I do love you, Andrea.

Prema Rose

Chosen Family

As an only child, something I always wanted was a sister, so what I seem to have done through the years is more-or-less turn my best friends into substitute sisters. It has been fairly easy to do this, because my chosen sisters didn't have any blood sisters either even though they had brothers.

And usually the sister bond was recognized and spoken about as such. I feel that this added dimension of friendship has been almost as important as the original friendship itself. I think that whatever one can do to cement and define a relationship adds another satisfying dimension to it. I have had three such sister-friends, one of whom is, sadly, deceased, but the other two I've known and valued for many years.

Longevity, as one of the benefits of this kind of friendship, may even be the best part, since it is the opportunity to choose one's family. And a same-sex family member is something of extreme value when one is chosen, perhaps as much as one's original family. Love is, of course, the other primary benefit...put together with longevity these two characteristics make life itself more of a thing of value. It's like adding flowers to one's emotionally heart-felt garden, something both friends can help to flourish and care for through the years.

Linda Holbrook

To My Sister-Friend

It wasn't the wine talking when I called you "sister" the other night. I really meant it. It was a year ago, that you showed up in my life. The day we met, I asked you that one little question: "Hey, do you want to see a movie sometime?" Because of that one little question we became friends.

Cocktails at an Italian restaurant and we bonded like two school girls. You were still reeling from your break up and me hardly knowing a soul in town.

We've shared our stories – happy and sad. You cried on my shoulder about how you'll never get married, and I recounted tales of my impossible boyfriends. We have traded healing work and even led a women's group together. You have shown up and supported me in my successes like my blood sister never could. No it wasn't the wine talking. You do feel like a sister to me. And, hey Sis, do you realize we have never ever seen a movie together?

Marcella J. Lively

Sister Brew

There are so many varieties of sisters, each as unique as women are themselves. As one who can extend the term "sister" to pretty much any woman, I have a single birth sister, and many, many more "Sisters". Every sisterhood bond is a blend of complex content - with the proportion of trust and distrust being one of the primary base ingredients.

My relationship with my birth sister is an unchanging, annoyingly stable concoction of difference, duty, control, and conditioning, fused together by a surprisingly determined devotion.

In contrast, chosen sisterhoods have a wider palate of colors and flavors - more juice, more spice, they become a true smorgasbord of shape, taste, and aroma. They may contain a wild psychotropic or two, for maximum potency and power. A vial of sacred tears is almost always included. The blends of these sisters are lovingly heightened by nurturing heat, gentle stirring, sometimes a long ferment. Exotic salt, fiery peppers, a touch of bitter, flowers, sweet cream - the abundance of the Goddess, that's what's on this platter.

Barbara McDaniel

Her Invisible Friend

Janda was my sister's invisible friend. Sometimes we had an extra chair at the dining room table for her. I had no inkling or clue or image of such a friend growing up. To this day Janda is in our conversation and I am more curious now in our late 70's about the nature of things unseen in my sister's life.

Last week she said to be on the lookout for something already on its way. And this morning I opened a nicely packaged box to find a blender bottle from Janda with the inscription, "something for our imbibing together while in Santa Fe." This August, we will be spending a week listening to opera, each of us coming from different parts of the country.

How does the energy of a 5-year-old invisible friend last over 70 years?

Ann Griffin

Precious Memories

Growing up in a family of five sisters and three brothers was challenging to say the least. I was one of three in the middle. The oldest sister, Rosa was easy going. Not a threat to my high energy. Her requests were easily ignored.

Second oldest sister, Grace, was another story. Her temper matched mine, I being younger would end up with the back of her hand across my head! Third sister, Betty was easy going and seventeen months older than I. There is no memory of the two of us fighting. There probably were disagreements but we seemed to settle them without trying to kill each other. Della was the third middle sister, two years younger than me. Also easy going until she wanted something then she was like a dog with a bone and wouldn't give up until she got it. The baby of the family was Karrol. We all loved her. Couldn't do enough for her as she was so little and cute.

As the years rolled by each of us went our own way. Rosa, our oldest sister moved away from home and married twice. Both husbands were losers. She was the one to keep their family together. She was a hard worker. With the second marriage, a son was born. She loved her church. Loved to sing. A precious memory of her is washing and drying dishes together. She washing me drying and singing to make the job go faster. Rosa died in 1992 of cancer. She was 62. The most amazing thing about Rosa, was that she knew she was dying long before the rest of us. She never earned that much with the job she had, but was able to save enough money each payday to pay for her funeral.

Grace our second oldest sister, never married, stayed home with Dad and Ma until they both passed away and then took care of Grandpa Bradley until he died. She then took a Nurse's Aide class and also learned to drive and got her driver's license so she could drive herself to and from work at a nursing home. She died at age 69 of breast cancer. After many years of not liking each other,

▶

Grace and I became good friends. I would call her on the phone and we would chat for at least half an hour. She caught me up on all the latest gossip around our little town. I miss her.

Betty and I were just 17 months apart. We thought alike. And were good friends, shared the walk to school every day through grade school, junior high and high school. Even had some of the same teachers. A tyrant gym teacher. Everything had to be regulation. Dark blue shorts, white blouse, black shoes. Neither of us could afford the full set of clothes for her class. We did the best we could, it wasn't good enough and our grades suffered.

During the summer of my sophomore year, I worked for a young family, baby-sitting and house cleaning. They lived on a farm, asked if I would like to stay on with them and go to school there. It was a different school district. I said I would. It was the best decision I have ever made as I met my future husband.

In the meantime, Betty worked for a young family, who also lived in the country, however the school Betty went to was our same school in our home town. She took the school bus into town every day. She had weekends off, I had every other weekend off. We would meet in town on my weekend off. The money earned during the week would be burning a hole in our pockets. It was spent wisely as we didn't earn that much. Later in the evening we would walk Main St. just to see how many boys were cruising Main and to see if they would whistle at us! Pretending to be offended by the whistling! But secretly enjoying it! What fun!

When Betty graduated from high school she moved to Rockford, Ill. I remember feeling so alone without her. We kept in touch by writing long letters back and forth.

I married and we lived on the old Carpenter farm for three years. Our three oldest kids were born in Iowa, then we moved to Colo. In 1961. Betty wasn't married yet and came to visit that first summer. She married a wonderful man in1963. They had two girls. We kept the letters going back and forth. During our yearly family reunions, we discovered we bought the same shoes, pants or top. Even living over two states apart, there was still that 'sister connection'. One family reunion, I remember telling her how much I liked her shoes. Her reply was, 'I'm glad you like them.' She handed a shoe box to me. Inside was the same shoes she had on!

Betty's youngest daughter, Karen, became handicapped and in a wheel chair for several years. Betty took care of her until Karen passed away in 1991. It was just a few short years later that her wonderful husband had a stroke. He became well enough to come home needing a cane and eventually a walker. He had seizures that would happen if he became over tired or stressed. Betty took care of him for around 10 years. He passed away in 2008. We are now at the point in our lives where we talk again on the phone, long three hour conversations. What a great way to keep in touch!

The memories of the years keep coming back to me. How many times had we jumped rope together? Played jacks? Something as ordinary as putting a puzzle together, or Chinese checkers. I never was able to beat Betty in Jacks or Chinese checkers! A precious memory I have is sitting on the floor playing Jack's. When it was Betty's turn, the ball would go up and she had a way about moving her scrawny fingers to pick up every one of those blasted jacks and still have time to catch the ball in that same hand without dropping a single jack! I knew I was the loser!

Della is the sister two years younger me. When young, she was very shy and didn't talk much. However by the time she was in her teens she had plenty to say. She loves music. In high school, she learned to play the clarinet. Della was also in the marching band. Della had girlfriends who loved to roller skate. If my memory serves me right, she would go to the roller rink with them. They would go roller skating every Friday or Saturday night. Della met her husband there as he loved to roller skate too. They married, had five kids. Mark, the middle son, died last year of pancreatic cancer.

▶

After her kids grew up and moved away she took the nurse's aide class and worked in nursing homes for several years. Her husband was a farmer and in later life worked as a mail carrier. Both retired. They moved to town and spend winters in Texas. Della and her husband Gene love to dance to country music. This last winter Della had serious health problems and the dancing has been put on the back burner until she is better. Della is an excellent cook and prepares meals so good one would think you had gone to heaven! We send emails back and forth as often as we can. If we lived closer, we would most likely go shopping together. Both of us love to shop.

Karrol is the youngest of the sisters and the baby of the family. She is eight years younger than I am. When she was very young she was small for her age and didn't eat much like the rest of us did. She is very intelligent. While in high school she worked for a lawyer as his receptionist. This was her after school job. After graduating high school, Karrol went on to a Bible college and graduated. Later she married her husband, whom she met at Bible College. They will soon be celebrating their 49th anniversary. They were blessed with two kids, a son and daughter.

As a teenager, she would come out to the farm where we lived and help me with housework and watch the kids while I would mowed our huge lawn. The grass had to be mowed once a week during the summer. It took a whole day. Karrol admitted to me several years ago that she wouldn't have known how to make a bed if I hadn't been for my showing her how. I thanked her for telling me. Karrol discovered she had breast cancer in 1992. She had that breast removed and in 2001 had the second breast removed. She eats healthy and loves to take long bike rides around the beautiful lake that is in their town. Karrol is an excellent organizer. Works at night at a home for very handicapped adults. Karrol has a great sense of humor and loves to tell funny stories that actually happen to her. She loves her church and is a faithful member. She would have made an excellent minister. One precious memory was of Karrol and our youngest brother Leo taking two of our cats to town for an animal parade. One of the cats didn't survive the ordeal as the day was steaming hot and as kids never think ahead that the cats would need water. Both kids were very sad for a couple of days. They were only four and five years old.

These are just a few of my Precious Memories. We were all blessed with angels watching over us.

Marie Carpenter

Branches

This lonely hot day
In a field of roses
There stood a tree
With many branches

She was old
And stood alone
A symbol
Of all things rare

Her branches spread
So far and near
That no one dare
Approach

Should she stand alone
With Strength, Hope
Endurance
To be herself

Or is it is worth
The time it takes
To be with sisters who
Have time to share

Marietta Harris

Relative
(Lyrics)

You have never known me,
    or taken my will
        from me.

Sister, you have never really
looked at me,
how can you call me
    like you
        know me
when you don't
      really
        know me—
or my home
      in a pasteboard
          box?
My glue
    upsets
        you,
land outside
    the wet
        flapdoor
          rot;
not mine,
    not yours,
either,
nor would you
      give it
to me free
    if it were.

▶

Sister,
  no,
    you don't
       know me
you never tried
      to find us
or looked   in behind us
    to find the
       pot we lived in,
so near
and so far from you;
you will   flower
without me,   beside me
      never me,
you will push your
    dirt in,
      and then
you'll ne-ver
    remember
that I'm in there
    with you;
      my babies
cry   to you
"Oh please, let me breathe,"
and will you
    give them
      air?
No.
  Because
    I won't let
      you.

Sis, oh, Sis,
    yes, Sister,
oh, yes,
  you call me;
you call me

SISTER
in public, though
        it's just for show.
You call me
     sister.
You call me
     sister.
You call me
     sister.
Forgive me
    if I can't
      answer.
No, don't
And I know
    you won't.

Trish Lindsey Jaggers

For You

i thought it was temporary...
i believed that family - familiarity could
overcome ANYTHING, because we
seemed to have been through
almost EVERYTHING
on this earth that is unspeakable
as innocents.

when i look up, at the stars, the
beautiful, beautiful spaces of light and life
in the magnificent skies, and of course the glory of
my ceiling, and the stars i have placed there
the warmth all comes back...
our life, my moments of recollection, feelings of
my simple and few recollections...oh...
some few memories of the thens...

i can't remember SO many things
i can't or don't have the recollections...
i wonder where they have gone
i THOUGHT i have supported
you, i know i may have wanted
to "fix" you, to comfort you, to let
you know that it was all ok...because
we were together...as sisters, as family,
sharing the best of
the worst.

it is an apology for what i may not know
i have done - and a reclamation for what
i have done that i do not know..
and, with some healing, those things
i know i did with intent
not to harm or remove myself, yet

▶

with accountable boundaries...
the distance of familiarity is the
most painful of all, save my one blood
seed of my life...a daughter...
life springs...

what a blessing...
always and ever more..
my darling vp...you go girl...
this cricket above me says he is
For You
living for the here and now. i
congratulate him/her on perseverance.
i am wandered and squandered on my
pettiness...oh great spirits...help me
through the next boundary.

i offer myself up to you.
i will get my things in order.
share the goods! there are so many who
do not have.
with all gratitude to you, GREAT SPIRITS...

Curtine Metcalf

Ode to Sisterhood

a prayer
to meeting and being met
wholeheartedly
sister pilgrims
making our way as best we can
through this world
this life
now by now
found so long ago
now lost
almost found again
but alas
now only lost forever
all the love laughter tears
vanished
disappeared
buried in a treasure chest
fathoms deep beneath the ocean floor
memories and future memories
that might have nourished us
for years to come
now toxic
never to be discovered
no hope to be recovered
I fully mourn the loss
and place it on the altar of my heart
wash it clean
and still pray for it to be redeemed

Dakini Lynn Marlow

Once I Was a Sister

I never had a sister
but
Once I *was* a sister
to my younger brother
but
He left too soon ......

My brother Curtis – Curt as he liked to be called – died in 2002. His shoes lived in my closet for years after that. They were White Stag, size 12W, black, men's dress shoes like a guy would wear with a suit only he wore them with everything.

I had been looking at them every day after he died and sometimes I would put them on just to see how my feet felt in them and to try to imagine how his feet felt inside them. Were they comfortable? Did they make his feet sweat? Where did he walk in them? To work? To the doctor's for sure. To the grocery store? To Mom's house?

What thoughts and feelings did he have when he was wearing them? When I looked inside I could see the imprint of his toes, although they no longer smelled like his

He always took his shoes off when he came in the house. The soles are worn in the same ways the soles on my shoes are worn, so I think we must have had a similar walk. Curt was born pigeon toed so he had to wear his shoes on the wrong feet for his first year to help the toes to turn back outward.

When Curt was a teenager we made a path using large concrete footsteps in ouryard. They were about 16 inches long. The neighborhood kids would ask if Curt had made those footsteps and they called him the Jolly Green Giant.

▶

Through the years his shoes have given me comfort when I open my closet. I could imagine him standing there in those shoes and on some level I could feel as if he was still there.

Then one day I looked at his shoes all dusty sitting next to my Merrills and I thought what a shame it was that they were trapped in my closet rather than being worn by some guy who had somewhere to go. Collecting dust in their creases and being locked up seemed like a poor substitute for being worn, enjoyed, polished and maybe complimented. I had just read something about how all things – humans, animals and objects – need to perform their function. Otherwise it's some kind of energetic unfulfillment. Besides, I thought, Curt is not coming back here no matter how long I keep his shoes.

So I picked up the shoes, took them downstairs and cleaned and polished the leather to a soft shine. I put them in a plastic bag and drove them to the clothing drop at Clarksville Reformed Church, where I said good bye to them and whispered a prayer that someone would be happy to have them. He walked on the earth in those shoes, but they didn't keep him here.

I still have his flannel shirts to snuggle into. And yes, Curt, I know your shirts are not you either. I visit with you now in dreams where you wear a lot of navy blue robes and I 'm so grateful for that my little brother with the little boy grin. I don't have to give you up. You walk with me still.

▶

Walking the Labyrinth

I walked the labyrinth with your hand in my pocket
and your voice on my shoulder.
Your shoes walked with me
and we saw that there are barriers in life
that you can jump sometimes if you want,
but if you do you find yourself someplace
you were supposed to be earlier or later

The smoothest way in or out is to follow the path
without leaping the stones, though you know you can
where the way of return is not what you think
and is unrecognizable, although it mirrors the way in.

If you don't follow the path you could be lost in the maze.
I heard your voice say" It takes a lot of patience, but
what else are we here to do, except follow the path to its end
where it begins again, notice what's in our way
breathing, opening, paying attention."
I say "I'm so happy to have you on this path with me,
so glad you return when I call
you, and wistful when you go."
"Tell me a truth", I say to you
"Tell me what you've learned over there
after you finished the labyrinth."
"Things just are" you reply. "Just look and enjoy,
there is nothing else to know."

Carole Fults

44

Friends

I always enjoy it when a new friendship is beginning which has the potential of becoming a different kind of relationship, one which will ultimately become more like a sisterhood.

I will, for example, never forget the fun and enthusiasm of the beginning of my friendship with Mary Claire when we were twelve and started high school in Atlanta. I think we both needed that friendship as we progressed from grammar school and its comforting smallness to the largeness of high school. We were like life rafts for each other in a big new sea. This friendship progressed to the extent that we decided we were the sisters each other had never had.

We even sealed the designation of sisterhood by having a Native American ceremony where we cut our index fingers and tied them together with a scarf to connect for what she fairly recently called "the mixing of our DNAs". So, there was no question as to the depth of our friendship which manifested itself in so many wonderful and unique ways through the years. And, now that we are 75 we are still close, and we enjoy reminiscing about all our good times together. We have a history and a bond which will undoubtedly remain strong for the rest of our lives.

Linda Holbrook

Bead for Life

For Betsy

Orange sunlight
color of beads on a necklace you craft
from paper found in dump yards
wet from street water dried in mid-day heat
molded carefully painted
strung for sale to afford school
since age five you chant
paper paper make me over

In Uganda you live close to killing fields in southern Sudan
mass graves destination place for young girls
dumped as paper you find to craft beads
pennies earned will be your machete
through wetlands of abuse
I wear the necklace chanting with you
Paper paper make me over

Barbara Truncellito

My Sister

My sister responds to my calls.
My sister laughs at my humor.
My sister listens to my joys and sorrows.
My sister boosts my self-esteem.
My sister lifts my spirits.
My sister accepts my faults.
My sister provides me with a safe haven.
My sister believes in me.
My sister loves me ... with no exceptions.

Diane L. Akins

Leaving Home

I realize the buffer I had been for my sister. She had always looked up to me. Whether I wanted that or not, that was how it was.

My job in the family structure had been to be smart, be observant, and mentally wrestle my father's energy to save my sister and my mother from having to deal with his confrontative behavior.

As I left home, my mother and sister grew even closer and aligned themselves against my dad. Now my sister had to deal with him directly, even though my mom was her ally. A great deal of arguing and emotional heat ensued.

I was sixteen, pregnant and moving into my boyfriend's parent's house, of fairly devout Catholics. My sister was thirteen and right on the edge of her own maturing process as a woman, suddenly the oldest and only child.

At the time, none of this registered. I was immersed in my own situation, stepping into a totally different world. I never thought about what I left behind and how my sister grappled with the family on her own until many years later.

Sometimes in conversation she referred back to that time as a painful place.

"Oh, when you left home and left me to deal with Mommy and Daddy," she'd say.

Because there seemed to be blame attached to it, as if I did it deliberately, I didn't think about it because it wasn't true.

Suddenly pregnant at sixteen and having to tell my mother, get married and move out, my own demons claimed me night and day.

It's only now in later years that hindsight brought the light of understanding to me.

Jyoti Wind
reprinted from:
Dreaming It Was Real:
A Childhood Memoir

The Scar

I grew up with brothers; there was no sister to compete with, no one to whisper to at night about boys, periods and pimples.

The dynamics of a sisterless girl in a family of boys toughens the spirit; forces the timid soul to become independent and strong.

This, coupled by frequent moves from one town and school to another brought me outside myself. I learned to make friends easily and quickly, and to move on emotionally with every new adventure.

In truth, I allowed few people into my inner sanctum. My heart was a strong fortress with buttressed walls and sturdy doors. Upheavals and challenges were obstacles to overcome, and I thrived on them as I moved from city to city, job to job and finally, leaving the country of my birth. I realized then that my whole life had been preparing me for foreignness. I would always be the new person, and here, I was the one with the accent. It didn't bother me.

My family was far away. At first I suffered homesickness but I hid it under a pretense of laughter. Brothers, for the most part, are not a specie that communicates well. Phone calls to my mother - bless her soul - were the only way I could remain connected to their lives.

Then the unthinkable happened.

A desperate phone call late one afternoon. I knew it was late for my mother to call. Something must have happened.

One of my brothers had been murdered.

I was on the plane going back to my family in Africa the next day. I had to be strong, very strong. Neither of my other two brothers could make it to the funeral. One was stuck in rural Malawi, the other, a surgeon, had operations scheduled that could not be postponed.

There was no time to cry, not time to grieve. I had to be stronger than that; I had to carry the grief in my heart, be a pillar of strength.

It was one of the most difficult things I have ever had to endure. It still is.

When I returned I felt broken.

But the spirit of generosity, the amazing American heart, opened to me. Friends rallied around me, embraced me and sustained me. I had finally found my sisters, here, so far from home and family. They surrounded me with their love, their nurturing, healing love. They understood when there were tears in my eyes. They felt my silences in the midst of chatter. An embrace, a hug, a glass of wine. And laughter, plenty of laughter, the universal band-aid. But it was more than that, it was the ineffable goodness, the unstinting generosity of their love that sustained me.

There is a scar still, but it doesn't hurt when you touch it. Not too much, anyway.

Christine Price

The Queens of 2nd Street

Before suburban sprawl, before the mall and big-box stores were built east of town, Casper, Wyoming was a small town where kids could roam safely long after dark. The downtown action was concentrated near the intersections of two streets, 2nd Street and Center Street. The Rialto Cigar store, next to the Rialto Theater, occupied the prime, corner location.

The cigar store sold a limited inventory of sundries besides tobacco products: magazines, newspapers, candy bars, and cokes that were hand-mixed from cola syrup and a carbonated soda dispenser.

Second street was a people watcher's paradise until around eleven o'clock, when the theater closed. Every parking place on the street would be filled: sedans full of families, the kids dripping ice cream from melting cones; trucks full of raucous boys in from the ranch for a few illegal cans of Pabst Blue Ribbon or Schlitz; couples snuggling in coupes or convertibles. Everyone was there to either see or be seen.

Once the cigar store and theater was shuttered, and the bars on Center Street dimmed their lights, the streets became silent, with only a few late night strollers–or an occasional car–to disturb the hush.

On one such night, around midnight, my friend, Jane, and I clattered down the middle of 2nd Street, defying nonexistent traffic, in ridiculously high-heeled shoes. I clattered louder because I'd bought a pair that sported a wooden heel and platform. I have no idea why they appealed to me at the time since they were amazingly unwieldly and caused me to walk with a stomping motion on the uneven asphalt.

Jane's shoes pinched, but she laughed with delight as we aimed for a cross street, six blocks away. At sixteen, even blisters can be funny.

▶

"Do you think anyone has seen us?" she asked. "Nobody, but nobody is wearing high heels with capris. We probably look like we're from California."

"Yeah. I know. Hollywood."

It was true. No one was wearing anything but ballet flats with capris that year in Casper.

To make it even better, we were among the very few girls in the high school who didn't favor long hair. We'd deliberately cut our hair short–not over two inches anywhere on our heads. I looked around and nearly twisted my ankle when I took my eyes off the pavement.

"A car went by a few minutes ago. I think it had boys in it."

"Wow," Jane said, "I bet they never seen anything like us."

They probably hadn't. We were dressed in identical clothes except for my wooden heels. I was a relatively tall brunette; Jane was a short blonde with broad, Finnish features. We'd picked out our outfits with care: formfitting, faux-zebra skin capri pants topped with oversized, men's shirts in an odd shade of salmon. We wore them with the tails hanging out and flapping around our upper thighs. We resembled flamingos more than starlets.

Jane thrust out her small chest. "I feel like Queen Shit herself," she declared.

"Me too," I said, "this is so cool."

"We are so cool," said. She smiled so broadly her cheeks looked like two apricots.

▶

We strutted down the street, swinging non-existing hair–and clearly existing hips–like we owned the world. We boldly challenged the entire town to look at us. On that September night, as we shouted and laughed our uneven way down 2nd street, we weren't working class kids from the poor side of the tracks. Jane wasn't slinging hash after school and weekends, in a greasy spoon restaurant on the outskirts of town, to support her mother and two young sisters. I wasn't the girl who'd lied about her age and gone to work, at age 13, in the local five and dime store. No. We were bold. We were beautiful. We were untouchable. We were the queens of 2nd street.

Jennie L. Brown

My Loving Sisters

She was the first, the beginning of my lifelong association with "sisters." My first cousin, my champion, and the one I'd imitate for the rest of her life. She's gone now, but forever will live in my memory, my heart, my soul. Dolores was her name, a talented, brilliant, fun-seeking being, so loving.

The second "sister" came into my life as my first cousin on Mom's side. Seven years younger, she looked up to me, imitated me, and loved me. She's gone now, but forever will live in my memory, my heart, my soul. Madelyn was her name, a happy-go-lucky, fun-seeking being, so loving.

Another "sister" appeared during high school, a tall girl like me, a brunette. My same age, we bonded immediately; she was the maid of honor in my wedding. She's gone now, but forever will live in my memory, my heart, my soul. Alberta was her name, a hard-working, caring, fun-seeking being, so loving.

Another high-school aged "sister" came along, a pretty, charismatic, short blond. She was deserted by her parents, and left in Denver alone, so adopted my family. She's gone now, but forever will live in my memory, my heart, my soul. Edna was her name; a live-wire who took dares seriously, a caring being, so loving.

In the hospital with my third child, a boy, my roommate became another "sister." We had many wonderful years together, traveled and shared our children's tales. She's gone now, but forever will live in my memory, my heart, my soul. Carolyn was her name, a mother of five girls, a laughing, caring being, so loving. She and I worked in the same department and discovered we were "sisters" at heart. We commiserated on our divorces and solved our mutual raising children alone problems. She's gone now, but forever will live in my memory, my heart, my soul. Alice was her name, mother of three, creative, caring, small but mighty, so loving.

▶

My other "sisters" are women from different areas: work, groups, and other places. We have wonderful times together, writing, picnics, pot lucks, luncheons, laughter. Each "sister" has a place in my heart, my soul. It's as though God picked them just for me. Ann, Arlotte, Bobbie, Cyndee, Diane, Elaine, Ellen, Janice, Jeannie, Joie, Julie, Shirley, I love you.

Beverly A. Simpson

The Preacher's Wife

When I was a child my mother began working with the local amateur theater. It gave her an artistic outlet that was missing in her life. Since she had divorced my father and I was an only child, I often spent a great deal of time at the theater. I often did my homework while sitting at make-up tables or under costume racks. I loved the place with its musty, dusty smells, and legion of friendly people. Mom ended up being the make-up director for most of the plays performed there.

The summer I was twelve I had been away with my father for a good portion of time on a trip "up north" to visit family. When I returned I discovered that my mother was working on a comedy titled "The Death and Life of Sneaky Fitch." A ticket was waiting for me for the Saturday matinée. The summer play was when teens were used to play the parts, so I was keen to see the performance.

I enjoyed the campy humorous take on the fictional Old West town of Gopher Gulch, but I had really zeroed in on the tall, willowy teenage brunette playing the part of the preacher's wife. The character was funny. Each time another character started to call ol' Sneaky "A low-down, yellow son of a – "she would pipe in with "pu-rarie dawg!" to keep the dialog clean. While she was funny, there was something else that drew me to her.

It was like I didn't know her, but I knew her. I recognized her, somehow, way deep down inside. It was eerie. The feeling stuck with me for months. Who was she? I had looked in the program. The name Betty Lewis meant nothing to me.

In the coming months my dad met a woman and by the next April I was walking into their wedding. It was just them and us kids -- her three sons and one daughter, and me. I entered the chapel at the church and there she was again – the preacher's wife. Within the hour Betty was my sister and I just couldn't believe it.

Life in a blended family isn't easy. Betty made it just a little easier for me by having known my mother before my dad and her mom even met. There was at least one person in this family who had known my mother without the bitterness my dad still held on to. She alone knew that my mother was a decent woman – with all the good and bad of any human.

After all these years Betty is still one of the coolest people I know and I admire her tremendously. I am grateful each and every day for the preacher's wife in my life.

Laurie Kay Olson

I Need the Eggs

If I had not taken a two year hiatus from the daily conversations with my sister, I most definitely would not be able to say anything resembling a coherent thought about our relationship. Truth is that until I disconnected some of the near pathological psychic intermingling between the two of us, she did nothing but drive me stark-raving mad.

Genius, artist, sensitive to any and all incoming stimulus, traumatized to the brink of insanity by my parents' cruel and demeaning treatment, drugged with Thorazine by age 5, displaced in the order of receiving love by the birth of my brother, the grief baby born on the day of my mother's father's passing, what can I say but that I get why she is the way she is, and yet too much contact and I feel entirely too close to the slippery slope of sanity as we know it.

I broke the silence by showing up to the 30th birthday she threw for her daughter. She rented a banquet room at a hotel. Catered a party for a hundred people. Ordered a towering stand of cupcakes, flowers on each table. The dj rocked the event. Wheelchairs were rolling. Walkers crowded the dance floor. My niece, still in diapers, decked out in her pink outfit and rosy lipstick all painstakingly chosen by my sister, communicating with a whisper or a bark, made the rounds of all her fellow fragile friends and their helpers. The most beautiful party I had ever attended. Not a dry eye in the house, some crying out of sheer ecstatic joy, others weeping for hearts breaking open, me by my sister's insistence that all events be celebrated in the grandest style, no matter your title. My brothers didn't show.

My sister and I are together again, but in the best way. As Woody Allen says in Without Feathers, a line he probably stole from a borscht belt comedian, or maybe this is how it is in all families, but when asked why he doesn't get help for his brother who thinks he's a chicken he replies, "We need the eggs."

Sunny side up, over easy, or scrambled, my sister is my eggs.

Order up!

Cindy Morris

Betsy

Betsy Fernie was born May 26, 1939, when I, her sister, was just 16 months old. According to our mother I was not delighted to have a little sister, and the only proof I have of her presence is in the many photos of the two of us together as toddlers. My memories of her came when we were older. I continued to be the Big Sister until she was 10, and I came down with Polio. She remembers thinking that she had to take over that role and be in charge since I was no longer able-bodied.

Before that time Betsy was very shy and fearful of anyone who came to our door. I remember her running upstairs and hiding under her bed when Mr. Quanstrom, the carpenter who built our house showed up. He was missing part of a finger, and she was fearful of strangers.

We shared a bedroom growing up and used to sing songs lying in bed before sleep after our mother had read us a story and tucked us in. She could carry the harmony. Wait Til The Sun Shines Nellie and Sisters were favorites.

By the time she got to junior high school, she began to come out of her shell. In High School she was a cheerleader, performed a solo drum dance for an all-school event, was very active in extra-curricular activities and a top student.

Betsy graduated from the University of Kansas where she met her husband, George Washington (Buzz) Hunt. She had three boys over 5 years and lived in Newport, Rhode Island while Buzz was in the Navy. She and I reconnected when I came to visit on weekends off from my job in NYC. I loved those beach-filled days playing with these rambunctious boys, my first nephews.

Her dream was to live in Colorado, so after a few years they built their dream house in the mountains west of Boulder and Betsy helped support her family, working in a doctor's office. Betsy loved being a mom, and they took trips in their VW camper to Canyonlands among other places. Nature continues to be her "church", and she hikes every week, renewing herself in the out-of-doors.

She lost her middle son, Peter when he was just 21 in a skiing accident in New Zealand on his rite of passage trip around the world. Betsy and Buzz divorced after 47 years of marriage and Buzz died a few years later.

Despite the heartbreak, she rides the waves of her life – the storms which took her strength and commitment, and the calm and courage that followed. She has been able to gracefully change course, finding the way using her own compass.

Betsy is a devoted grandmother to her three grandchildren and has a wide circle of close friends with whom she shares her life, her generous spirit and a lot of travel adventures. And she spends one day a week with me to help out. She is once again the big sister, since I am unable to carry out all the tasks I once did because the ghosts of polio are revisiting my body. I am delighted and blessed to have my sister in my life once again. We share gatherings at our family cabin, good food and stories, and sometimes we might burst into song, reliving those harmonies we once shared growing up on the Kansas prairies.

Susan Fernie

Storms in Africa

For the lost girls in Nigeria from their mothers

Let it storm
footprints in mud leave a trail
for one who weeps harder than rainfall
asks the hidden moon for my daughter

Classroom mourns her laughter her eyes wide
dreams swirling in vivid colors
as her head scarf caught in branches
of trees broken by her captors
who rape her to pass time
not as I who wrap her in caresses

Let the storm scream as I do
searching tracks in the mud
my last prayer.

Barbara Truncellito

Portraits

Thoughts are floating by as the
ripples in the stream I perceive,
and I see faded photographs
of yesteryear;
the most beautiful one I can discern
is of a friend whose joie de vivre
and violet eyes stunned me
with their light.

So bright, my memory can find
no fault in this fair friend;
a mere maiden at the time,
she must have loved Lancelot,
for no one else would have been
knight enough for this Guinevere.

It seems that her birthday was near
mine, and I thought that simply had
been planned, for we were so much
alike, we dreamed of life and love
together hand-in-hand;
some chance meetings, some meet
by chance, but we were like sisters
in the same circle and saw no end
to the high school dance.

Some portraits of the past
are as full as a wedding scene,
and time takers no toll on their gloss;
whether they are as a fine and fruitful
tree or endure an early frost,
nothing gained so fervently
ever can be lost.

Linda Holbrook

Circles of Sisters

Two little lion cubs - playing, biting, spitting, pouncing - either constantly in motion - or asleep. That is how I visualize the early childhood of me and my sister. I was born first, a fact that she is still rather resentful of, but then she did not taste the responsibility that being first-born carried; it wasn't always as good as it looked. Two little Leo girls born two years apart, looking enough like twins as we grew up that some folks thought we were. Today we are dear friends but it took us several years and some miles apart to mature into this more gracious connection.

And there are the circles of sisters with whom I have shared my adult life. Being outrageously blessed with amazing friends in this lifetime, I cannot imagine living through it without them. As I do not believe in coincidence, I marvel at the wide range of people that shared space with me.

My first circle formed in college where I lived on the eighth floor of a co-ed dorm, which in Missouri at that time meant the boys lived in one tower, the girls lived in another tower, and the two were connected in the middle by a large cafeteria where we were allowed to mingle over carbohydrates. Away from home and feeling brilliantly independent, I was in heaven. I began the long linage of sisterhood by friending myself with young women who lived on my floor. I was looking for new and exciting ways to celebrate life; they helped me frost my hair, pierced my ears, and my new roommate, an only child from St Louis, decided to teach me how to drink Scotch. Forty-five years later several of us still send each other Christmas cards and I, for one, look forward to their Christmas letters and family photos!

I made a road trip with one my college friends who had been invited to live out west! I fell in love with a man and the small rustic mountain town where he lived, and moved to Nederland, Colorado, right before my twenty-first birthday. It was in this

▶

heady, high altitude environ that we came together – women I have known and loved dearly now for over forty years – a circle that will never be broken. We were young hippy chicks looking for love and an alternative life style that would carry us beyond the boundaries set by our well-meaning, but perceived naive, parents. We laughed and called Nederland "the spiritual center of the universe." My mother cried and called it "the land of the losers." But as we women shared bottles of cheap wine, cried over lost loves and celebrated new romance, made plans for the future sitting in a hot tub drinking champagne, peed in the woods at the top of mountain passes, careened around the dance floor, or sat outside in a snow drift and howled at the moon - we cemented relationships that supported us through the decades that followed.

Time passed and we spread our wings and left the nest.

After not seeing one another for fifteen years, we planned a reunion. We all flew into San Francisco and spent a few nights exploring what I had always idolized as the birth place of my "inner flower child." We came together naturally and sincerely. It was as if we had left for work in the morning and gotten together for dinner that evening to share the remarkable aspects of our individual lives. We flowed into one another easily and gently; listening spell-bound at each one's personal adventure, or wildly holding five conversations at once in an ever increasing crescendo. It was an awesome adventure of re-connecting. Here we sat; business owners, women serving important functions for large corporations and non-profit organizations, mothers, home owners, married, divorced or single we had made lives for ourselves and achieved success in this lifetime. We were all winners !!

Our conversations were awesome and segued through the years we had actually been apart. We laughed as we realized it took all of us to quilt together pieces of our better parties. Our drug of choice was now dark chocolate Espresso beans. "Careful, too many and you will never sleep tonight. Tee hee !!!" We had a group photo taken under the street sign at the infamous 1500 Haight St & 600

▶

Ashbury. Seven smiling goddesses. We are very beautiful in that picture which still hangs on my bedroom wall.

And then there is the small circle of Hockey Mom's, and my horseback riding friends, and the lifelong friendships formed during a year of learning at the Rocky Mountain Center for Botanical Studies, and the healing circle I sat in for five years as we explored somatically, the energetic world we are living in. And more recently, the circle of my herd mates who have dived into the ever expanding world of equine gestalt coaching, bringing together my love for horses with the desire to be of assistance. Mostly my circles stand alone, but sometimes they overlap and that only deepens the attachment.

As I think of sisterhood, another little incident keeps pulsing at the back of my brain so it must be important to share it as well. I was at a department store many years ago with one of the original Mountain Mama's. We had graduated into careers and now had more money and less time, the direct opposite of our younger years. On this day my friend was purchasing mascara.

The sweet young woman behind the counter showed Shirley a slim wand and said, "This is the newest in the natural look. They will hardly know you have it on."

Shirley looked her straight in the eye and declared, "If I am going to buy this, take it home, and bother putting it on, I sure as hell want someone to notice!" I have laughed about that so many times through the years and believe it may sum up my life on this planet with these wonderful women, my sisters.

By golly, we went to the trouble of being born, the agony of growing up, the trials and tribulations of learning how to do relationship, and were not afraid – then or now - to show up and do what needs to be done.

We are absolutely worthy of notice !!

Annette Price

I Remember You

I remember you
with short blonde bangs
and a toothy grin
from ear to ear.
You tagged along with me
and friends.
As you grew
it was natural for you
to gather neighborhood kids
and play school.
I was on my Underwood
tapping out
the great American mystery
with you giggling
in the background.

You bought the hat at Easter
that came with a purse,
while I had a 6 gun
and boots on my feet.

Later we danced to doo-wop
the Pony, Twist, and Skip.
The same music
fed us both
but otherwise
we were so different.

You burned every summer
while I tanned.
You stayed blonde
while I darkened.
You never married
while I did twice.

▶

You went into the world
while I stepped aside.
You stayed home with parents
while I left.

Yet in final years
we met in the middle
of what life gave us.
We got closer somehow.
A wish my father
always had for us
that we would
appreciate each other.

We just had to grow
into it
and finally did.

Jyoti Wind

Sister Boss's Wife One

My boss's wife took pity on me, a young buck working in a foreign land for a monolithic and impersonal employer. She became my big sister even though she is somewhat younger than I. It was my first time away from home and without my mother's guidance and good counsel. God only knows how I might have gone astray had I not been taken in to my boss's wife's family and under her left wing.

I had met my boss overseas. I worked for a small group. He was the deputy boss. We bonded when we took an overnight train trip together. I got to our cabin earlier and claimed the lower bunk. He tap danced in moments before the train pulled out. He pulled rank on me and sent me climbing. We spent the first half of the night talking in the dark, vertical guy bonding. By dawn's early light we were friends for life, though we didn't know it at the time.
My boss and I referred to his wife as "One". The use of a number came from our organization's penchant for having groups count off to take attendance. Boss was Two. I was Three. Dog was four barks.

One and Two's relationship with me, Three, grew close over the years. They had me over for dinner many a time, mostly on weekends. One is a fabulous cook who eschews prepackaged or ready to heat and eats. She starts from scratch with basic ingredients. I tried to find scratch in a food emporium once but couldn't locate it.

We took vacations and traveled together with me and Four Barks sitting in the back of their Beetle. They decided where and when we would go and I always went there at then. I never had a problem getting the same time off as my boss. We shared expenses, but somewhat asymmetrically to my financial benefit. For example, I was never asked to pay for gas, what little their

▶

wheels consumed. I contributed by volunteering for petty chores such taking Four Barks for business walks early and late while we were on the road.

I was standing outside the delivery room when One gave birth to her first born, a daughter. The boss had been in the room with her. Three me was the third person to see the newborn, not counting the medical people facilitating the delivery. I took the first photos. When it was time for One to come home, she drove while the boss held the baby in the front seat of their bug. I leaned over between the bucket seats and shot a picture of him looking down on the precious little one. Light pouring in from the windshield and was washing over the baby while her dad's face remained in the shadows. It was one of One's favorite photos. One's baby grew up calling me "Uncle Bob."

Due to a series of lucky-me events that I still find hard to believe happened, I shortly thereafter found myself married to a bonnie lassie from another foreign country. I had been down on marriage as I'd never met a happily married couple in my clan. Even my parents constantly bickered. One and Two gave me hope. They were very happy. Based on that, I walked down the aisle and joined in a marriage that's lasted almost 45 years so far. Thank you, One.

The first time I brought my bride to meet One and Two things did not go well. One told me later about the mistake I'd made. She sensed my wife's discomfort as the three of us were so close. One told me to stay away for six months or so until we two newlyweds had bonded and could come back as a couple meeting another couple. What a sage woman One is, no! What a wonderful big sister!!!

My wife and I got to know each other in the hiatus sufficiently to create another soul. My boss was outside the delivery room when my wife gave birth to our daughter the next April. Two was the third person to see her. However, I was again the one taking the pictures. I caught the delivery room nurse in the corridor carrying our newborn to the nursery by going out the back door of the birthing room. I asked if I could take a photo and held up my Polaroid. She said, "One." I took it and I asked, "Should I send the photo to my mom or my wife's mom?" The nurse frowned and said, "Two."

We never gave my wife a number. To me she is a Ten, like in the movie.

It was a sad day when it was time for my spouse and me and to return to the United States. We were both homesick for the land of the round door knobs. We had had a fabulous time seeing a part of the world that others paid dearly to visit for a few days. We could drive to neighboring countries and still be home by dark. I would miss living there, but most of all I would miss One, my big sister. But fate wasn't done with us. After a series of moves, my boss and I ended up living close, but in neighboring states. We started a series of jobs for our employer writ large where most of the time he was in the head of a unit of which I was a member, albeit down the food chain a bit. Sometimes he'd move first and I'd follow. Other times I'd strike out and he'd catch up. One continued to sister me, but less frequently and more subtly as now I had a wife to tell me what to do.

When One's daughter had her first of two babies, I realized I'd eye witnessed a generation. I was there when the new mother was born out of One and now she was giving birth, twenty some years later. The thought had a profound effect on me as I realized two decades had passed by in a flash. It was the first inkling I had of my heretofore ignored mortality.

On another job change, the boss moved into our corner of our state. I continued to be in his orbit in the organization. We now were

▶

again taking vacations together, some for extended periods of time. I first realized that my Ten had bonded with One and Two when she'd began to choose to go with them when there were options for what to do on vacations. For example, the three of them are beachers, I not. He'd take the ladies to the water's edge. Landlubber I, I'd stay far ashore, high and dry.

My boss and I eventually retired. About this time there was a change in two important vectors in our lives. One and Two started vacationing with their grandchildren, now out of diapers. And Ten and I moved away, far away.

Although we are now within a long day's driving distance of each other, we've only gotten together once in the intervening years-- when we stayed with them overnight. How we let this happen is a mystery. I miss One in my life. She is a great wife, a wonderful mother, a doting grandmother, a fastidious housekeeper, a skilled cook, a dog lover, a baseball fan and my favorite sister. She's the One I love.

Bob Surrette

Silver Maker

I hear the thousand footfalls
of women who stood
beneath you—night
twisted about their feet
like asps—mouthing
shy whispers to you.

In your gaze, dark glows
silver like an amulet
cupped in the concave of your throat.

Your honey-glistened edge slices
the night curtain into the sweet
fringe of predawn.

No one has higher knowledge
of the conversations between us,
for you tell no one
our secrets, those secrets
we took before you,
on nights like tonight—
when the wind pulls its sandalwood
comb through strands of trees.

The grasses don diamonds for the occasion.
I pluck a handful and fling them to you.

You are the jeweler
for the sisters of the night,
and we wear your pillages
like kept women.

For we know the Silver Maker,
and She loves us.

Trish Lindsey Jaggers

Dear Sister,

So many days I look inside and notice a feeling of anticipation for our next phone chat with a joy of our reconnection along with tenderness and sympathy for the distance between you and your husband, especially when he says, "you are sleeping all alone in the bedroom and I'm all alone here." (in a care facility)

I am feeling renewed love for you everyday getting to know you have concerns at work and J's demands to come home. I feel with you in your tiredness at the end of the day, just as I am tired sometimes.

I mostly feel an appreciation for what we are weaving together with our mutual interests and with our upcoming visit.

And as I look at what I've just written, words like moved, touched, grateful, amazed, eager, interested, stimulating come to mind. Some parts of me feel restored and revived.

Who would have thought after decades of us being apart, I can so naturally live in these feelings.

Your Younger Sister,
Ann Griffin

76

My Soul Sistas

Are book savvy
Come together for tears and cheer
To share chocolate
Each digs for her answers
Shares individual wisdom
Eagerly received
Soulful conversations
Hold me captive to their thoughts
With focused interest
Never tiring
Of their happy chatter
Or serious talk
Welcome
Readily available
Heart felt hugs
Cherish sacred relationships
For each Intelligent Heart
Holds love space deeply within
For those reasons
Shared joy and respect
Coupled with gratitude for my Soul Sistas.

Charlene Ellington

My Soul Sistas and I belong to a long standing book club called
The Intelligent Hearts, who meet weekly.

The Broken Chord

Every cloud has a silver lining. A ray of hope in the darkness, a beacon that we can set our sails to in a stormy world.

Silver, so shiny; so precious. The Mother metal, the metal of the Goddess, the Creator Essence.

We are connected to each other by ribbons of silver light, and to Her, to feed our souls, to uplift our spirits. That is the color of friendship, connecting to the essence of the love that we have and share with each other.

How then, Celeste - how did our ribbon of light become so tarnished? It is covered in a film of pain, anguish and anger.

How does one color betrayal? What does it sound like? A misalignment of notes? A discordant inharmonious clash of bitterness in the soul?

Is that the sound I hear in those patches of black and grey? Is it that the sound in my heart when you stole him away?

I thought we were friends; no, more, far more than that? I thought we were soul mates, sisters - part of a greater whole that sang the same hymn, that floated together in the experiences and laughter we shared.

I know how to share: the giving of heart and soul, opening myself up to allow space in my innermost being for others. I did not know that you would abuse this generosity, Celeste.

But, I forgive you. I forgive you for we are each other's lessons in life. An opportunity to forgive. A time to love again. And as I pray for you, giving to you all the love I can hold in my heart, I see the ribbon begin to change. I hear the notes begin to harmonize.

The black turning to grey, the grey beginning to fade. Slowly, prayer by prayer, I begin to see bits of silver beginning to shine through again.

Yes, there is a silver lining. It lies in our forgiveness. Forgiving myself, for those were my feelings, not yours. I had tarnished the ribbon; now I will make it shine again.

I will sing my song to you once more - to you, to the creative power of Love.

For love, Love, that is all we can be.

Christine Price

Moth

Clinging to the wood between the panes
slowly fanning his soft brown cape
the grand silk moth just wanted shade
no one had ever seen a moth this large here
one told one and then another one a crowd
gathered to watch in silence her breathing
wings each long as my middle finger
that night I dreamt of my sister
with her large eyes and brown hair
dead these many years before this
with the silence of brown velvet breath
days later nothing where the moth had been
later still in her resting spot I saw a small
less than one inch in length
ghostly white moth with folded wings.

Claudia Chapline

Aunt Kathy

Aunt Kathy my kids called her. She was fourteen when my first son was born and seventeen when his brother followed. She loved the role. She came to babysit while my husband and I had a night out, here and there.

When I separated and took my two year old son home to family, she was there. I got a waitress job, she babysat and fed him dinner several nights a week. Without her, it wouldn't have been possible.

In her 20's, Kathy worked in an office for awhile and then on to restaurant management, with up-to-the-latest fashion and hair style. I was a stay-at-home mom. She bought fabric and a pattern for clothes that I would sew for her, and fabric of my choice for me. This way we both expanded our wardrobes.

Through the years, she never forgot the kids birthdays. Her own son was born, and still she remembered. When she became Great Aunt Kathy, she was great. She had gifts for my grandchildren at their birthdays and Christmas when possible. When they came to the Shore, she showed up with pails and shovels for the beach, animal pillows for sleeping, and always bagels and cream cheese for lunch.

She was a generous soul.

Jyoti Wind

Fiery Sister

We had a fiery sister, red-haired and prepared
to fight the high power cuz he don't 'low dancing and fun.
She ruined her Sunday clothes sliding down an icy hill.
We said, You're mad! you're bad! Stay in! Sit still!
I won't like a god who won't like me! she said.

No god exists or he goes secretly.
Let him step up and then I'll see. She said,
The moon is rock and fences make me sad.
We trembled at her blasphemy. We said,
You're mad! Now do keep still!

She shook her fist, tossed her red hair, set to best
the divine who don't 'low music all night long.
We said, You're bad! You'll shake the town!
You'll sink us down with what you're thinking!
What wildness gives you such a thrill?
Come, get off the windowsill!

We wore her down. One day she snapped,
said, God is good so I'll be good. The moon
is cheese and fences please. Got on her knees—
snipped off her hair. Her hands and mind she folded,
consenting to be shorn to belong.

We were glad, no longer scared,
comforted by her capitulation.
We sat at table, one eye on our bread,
the other ceiling-ward, quite sure he don't 'low folks
all playing run sheep run outside the pen.
Baa baa, we said, enfolding warmly our cosmetic sister
who was willing to be broken to belong.

Patricia Lapidus

82

I Got A Call the Other Day

I got a call the other day
from a lady unknown to me, a total stranger on the line
Linda is dead, she said.

Jumped from her 7th story apartment balcony
Splattered below, in broken pieces
coroner came, scooped up what was left
She was no more

Apartment is emptied; ashes have been scattered
No body to view, no questions to sort, no questions answered
Linda is gone

My mom informs me my Dad is struggling
with what he *may* have done to contribute
Linda jumped on Father's Day, could have been an indicator?
Or incest, violence, abuse, hatred of kids...
Hmm...Perhaps...Struggling...Doubtful

What is family? What was family?
An only sister with no contact for over 7 years?
Not seen for 16?
A Mother who wants to know when I will be reconciling with my
Father?

Linda planned this, the lady said
Since February, at least, "How to" books by her bed
No machines for her, no half-ass attempt
She got it right

I got a call the other day
from a lady unknown to me, a total stranger on the line
Linda is dead, she said.

Karen Stewart

Brat on Record

Sara, my only sister, is nearly ten years older than I, and is the eldest. Our three brothers are middle children, and I'm the baby of the family. We four younger siblings were the conspiring forces who robbed the first born of her "only child status." Sara reminded us of that fact with one-liners like, "I had it good until you guys came along."

Growing up, I looked up to Sara and hoped to connect with her on a meaningful level. But the age difference between us was much like two positive poles of a magnet; we were born from similar cells, and our life forces repelled each other. On rare occasions, an invisible wire device merged our currents.

In 1964, I was a play-in-the-dirt six year old, when Sara turned into a moody sixteen year old. Sara owned a hi-fi phonograph that played 45's and LPs. The modern two toned orange and white portable had a penny taped to the stylus. Voices of pop artists like the Jan and Dean, Dave Clark Five, and The Beatles blared from the same speaker as the instruments. Granted, the songs played on the radio, but the record player bestowed a freedom to choose when to hear a song, and unless scratched, records were static free.

With the fifteen cents I got from the tooth fairy, I bought a stack of 45's at a neighborhood garage sale. The fact they were older tunes mattered not, because they were mine. Sara listened to each one and scolded me for trying to copy her, "These are dated songs. Not the latest hits disc jockeys play on the AM dial."

Unless Sara found a need for me, I was no more than her bratty little sister unworthy of notice. Until one day, opportunity arose for a special interaction. Sara planned to attend a school dance and deemed it necessary to practice the moves. To my delight, she used me as a partner and taught me how to dance. In truth, I needed very little instruction as I had learned many of the steps from watching

American Bandstand on TV. We actually had fun together playing Sara's records on the hi-fi. We wiggled and shook to the twist, the monkey, the jerk, the mashed potato, and the swim.

The glory that filled the moment ended abruptly, and I returned to my role as the "pain in her ass." Our relationship deteriorated to the point she called me a little devil.

Why? I could not keep my hands of her records. In defense, I blamed Sara for my naughty behavior. Hopelessly bitten by the rock and roll bug, I snuck into her room repeatedly, set the needle on the vinyl, and played the broom like a guitar strumming maniac. The cat retreated to the closet while I sang into a brush. As if possessed by the beat, I danced as if my soul caught fire. I was alive!

Sara continually pushed me away as she dangled her affection, and everything she owned, in front of me. Her seductive attitude, "Ya can't have it because it's mine," only fed my temptation to touch and feel her golden treasures. Things like her floral makeup bag, and penny collection book were far more exiting than my plastic dolls. Repeatedly, she laid into me for trying on the make-up and rearranging the locations of the coins.

"Keep your grimy mitts off my stuff, you little shit," she spat daggers.

The pain of her words stabbed at my heart. Yet persistent as an unwanted fly, I continued to venture into the land of intrigue until she fastened a padlock to her bedroom.

Months later, Sara softened, allowing me to watch her apply brow pencil without shooing me away.

I asked her, "Why are you getting so dolled up?"

▶

"Gonna get myself a boyfriend," Sara replied. She already combed out the shampoo set and teased her hair until it poofed a couple inches above her head. Her auburn quaff flipped up at the ends and rested on her shoulders.

"None of your business," she said in voice that told me to press no further.

"What's the big deal?"

"You're such a blabber mouth. You tell mom everything. Now scram. You're bugging me," Sara scolded.

The big sister rejection was loud and clear. It left me praying, that some day, Sara might like me. Waiting felt like an eternity.

Sara left home and married when I was eight years old. Our lives unfolded by default. Within a year, she became a mother, and found me useful as a free babysitter.

We remained distant, unable to be each other's confidant. A cousin my age and friends provided that intimacy.

I became bored raising my nephew on weekends while Sara partied. She offered to pay me at the end of the summer when she and her husband intended to sell their car.

Their refurbished 1957 Chevy would be sellable by then. Convinced we had a deal, I gave my services all summer. I never saw a dime. Fed up from lack of respect, Sara and I drifted further apart. We rarely talked during my teen years. After high school, I moved a thousand miles away. Twice a year, on Christmas and Thanksgiving, she called me to stay in touch. There was no even exchange, I listened while Sara rambled a detailed monologue of her life, and literally hung up when she was done. Never did she want to hear my voice or ask anything about me. By then, I dreaded to hear her voice through the phone receiver.

Actually, not until age fifty-five, when our mother died from a stroke, and a month later cancer took our brother, did Sara and I connect on a meaningful level. The double whammy grief caused her to pause and listen to what I had to say. She feigned concern, and for the first time in my life, asked me how I was. Before she could dominate the airwaves, I said, "You have no idea who I am, do you?"

"How can you say that? You're my little sister who got into my penny book and make-up."

"I'm an adult now. Can you tell me what my hobbies are?" I asked.

"No." Sara faltered.

"If you're interested getting to know me, take a turn listening for a change."

Many tears fell between us. It took the shock of our mother's death for Sara to open her heart. With mom gone, the competition for maternal attention disappeared. The old mental tape that saw me as a little brat vanished. Our family dwindled down to two brothers, Sara and I. (Dad passed twenty-five years ago.) Inspiration awoke Sara's senses to view me as a newfound treasure. My prayers were answered, for we became friends.

Our belated closeness transformed our sisterhood beyond mere tolerance, because the crap between us decayed, and flowers grew above the ashes of our mother.

Holly Hunter

Our Stories Were Never the Same

We shared paper dolls, twirled
in blue tutus, savored sundaes,
chased fireflies at dusk. But
our stories were never the same.
No matter our intention,
there were things left unsaid.
No matter what our mother
told us, some wounds do not heal.
We chose to bury the tangled
skein of our sisterhood.
It wasn't until you lay dying
that I joined hands with your
Sufi sisters and learned
the Dances of Universal Peace.
Fourteen years have passed
since I washed your body,
brushed your tangled hair,
wiped you clean for the last time.
I imagine you beside me.
The scent of orange and ginger
fill the room. I want to believe
that you would choose me
as your sister again.

Leslie B. Neustadt

Sisters

To some of us sisters come late in life
growing up with an all-boy neighborhood
marrying; offspring of four sons, and a male dog
even my husband's business was male dominated
a mason contractor, employees gathered at the house

even my workplaces over the years
had all male bosses, truly encouraging
I broke loose of parental duties, marriages
opened my own dream business, a book shop

that's when I found sisters so dear to me without
any sibling rivalry, no growing-up pains, no petty
jealousies to grow out of, before bonding together

I found sisters in my closest women friends, we share
rituals, talking sticks, stories, written & oral, tears, and
accomplishments; we spread celebratory tables laden
with foods, wines, waters, and hand-holding words, sent
out into the universe to bring peace to the world and to us

bonded not by blood or family rules telling us what we should
but by womenhood, by shared experiences,
by the love of each other

Arlene Sandra Bice

No Saving To Be Done

There's no one left to save.
My parents have passed,
and I got the lesson
before they died.
There's no saving anyone
from the path
they came to walk,
even if to you
it looks like they need it.

With my sister,
I got caught again,
thinking she needed to move,
to come to a place
that had more consciousness
around life, food, spirituality.

But I thought about it
long and hard,
and knew it wouldn't matter
to her because it never had.

So I let it be
and she lived out what life she had
where she felt most comfortable.

There was nothing to save her from.
No saving to be done at all.

Jyoti Wind

My Russian Sisters

For the people of Ukraine

Nurses from Mother Russia
craft brought to me in my youth
you healed me with your hands
craft you learned in your studies

I remember your stories of life in Kiev
as stones toppling into a brook
overflowing with old speech and a new war

What do you see as you watch crowds cling past moonlight
stirring passions you thought lost
in passages of song and prayer
they reach for a new order
in cobblestones dancing in alleys
in your healing hands now clasped
watching the politicians play
elders of the Ukraine wait in silence

Barbara Truncellito

The Magical Days of Childhood Summers

In the early mornings, during summer's hottest days, we older girls, of the middle sisters, (there's five of us) would drag our old dilapidated wash tub out to the middle of the front yard where the sun would shine heavy and hot during the heat of the day. The three of us were perhaps seven, nine and ten. Having no long hoses like we have today, the tub would have to be filled with water from the well. We would take turns pumping the water into the only bucket while then taking turns carrying the bucket from the well to the wash tub. The water from the well was colder than water from a tap so it took longer for it to get warm. A good two to three hours.

I remember many times going out to test the water to see if it was warm enough. The temptation would be too great and I would have to throw some on the nearest person. Even if the water wasn't warm enough yet, that temptation would start a water fight! We would change into older clothes. However when someone like me who couldn't resist the temptation of starting the water throwing, wouldn't have had time enough to change.

Soon the sounds of laughter and screams would bring some of the neighbor kids in. Then the real fun began. Even though the water wouldn't be warm enough after getting wet, it felt so good cooling off in the heat of the day. Old blankets were spread out far enough away from the water throwing but yet in the sun. When we became too cold and shivery we would run to the blankets and lay in the sun until we were warm enough and brave enough to take another run into where the water throwing was taking place. Tin cans were the best to throw the water from. If there happened to be any water left, we would let the younger kids enjoy it.

It would be warmer by this time and they would sit in the tub and use the tin cans to pour it over each other. We would be so tired from running, laughing and screaming that it was a sure bet we would all have a good night's sleep that night, leaving us to dream of magical days of childhood summers.

Marie Carpenter

Three Sisters

We sisters three are identical, born minutes apart eighteen years ago.

Before we outgrew the identification bracelets place upon our arms at birth, our wise mother painted our big toe nails with a different color of polish. The polish corresponded with our names. My oldest sister, by twenty minutes, is Ruby Renee. Her nail was painted with Ruby Red polish. Gail Marie who is ten minutes older had a shade of polish that was Green Mint. As for me, the smallest of the three, I was given the longest name for a polish called Blue Sky. I am Bethany Samantha. This was not a fashion statement, but because it was just difficult to tell us apart.

Oftentimes through the years, when I was asked if I was Bethany, I would tell the person I was Gail. In turn, Gail would say that I was Ruby. On and on we'd go, having fun fooling people as to who we really were, and loving every moment of it.

Suddenly our big day arrived. Graduation from high school was a big event. As our names were called, we three proudly walked across the stage to receive our diplomas. Wearing sandals, our toes clearly displayed red, green and blue polish covering each of our ten toes.

As I glanced into the audience, I saw our mother with a smile from ear to ear.

Julie Ann Orecchio

The Late Sister

Rinse and repeat!
The last of the litter.
The late child who comes
before dessert is served.

What can you expect, really
when you parents wait for Godot,
the wind blows dust and wild
and you are the late late show?

Whose idea was it, you want to know
to stop making quaaludes before you
could ride the roller coaster, show up
drunk at the last stop on the metro?

"And where," you ask, "are the snaps
of me?" The black and whites, the
ones at the beach with cousins,
the dancing aunties, old loved dogs?

You came with rock and roll,
the tale's end, end of the boom
while I was out on the town
a traveler in another room.

Now we are orphans of the fall
We sit on the beach and call
our dogs, our children, our lives
to come back, to start again.

Here is what we know:
At night all birds are black
Everything we have we choose,
And one day, this life we both shall lose.

April Bennett Stone

Amanda

We met on a shore
licked clean by tides,
and we ran, sisters, untethered horses
with no shoes, sea-polished glass
between our toes,
journals in our hands.

You love morning glories,
their vines, how they tangle
into each other, how pulling one free
hurts the other. You, the offspring
of words, love how they rhyme
without trying, how they call you back
home, how home made us
leave and take it with us
on sheets now white with salt.

Your words a strand
of blonde tucked in a dark braid, heavy
over the marks
down a young girl's back.

Your first words
carved on the page;
they hurt, the cutter's blade,
but then, the scar—
oh, how we trace the scar.

Trish Lindsey Jaggers

Cinderella's Ugly Sister

She silently thought about it
murdering her little sister
with the big kitchen knife
to have everyone's attention
to have Mommy and Daddy
all to herself to have everything
to have but not to have
a sister sharing parts
that young one with dainty feet
enormous swimming-pool eyes
that's what she thought about
when she saw her sweeping

She thinks
my beauty comes from the inside
it glows through the holes in these rags
through the soot on my face
I do all the work and
you are so mean to me
even in those fancy clothes
you are still so ugly ugly ugly
I look down so I don't have
to look at your mean ugly old face
I want to fly up the chimney
and dance with the smoke
or a handsome prince

Claudia Chapline

My Three Sisters

I had three sisters, all named Amy.

I carried the first Amy home from Worcester Hospital half a century ago. After two boys and a dozen barren years, my Mother finally had given birth to the girl she'd always wanted, as she told one and all, making my brother and me feel like speed bumps in her life. For some reason I've never understood, I naturally took to childcare. Perhaps I had some chromosome cross channel confusion.

It was win, win, win. My stressed mom was happy to have the help at home. My sister, and the final brother that followed Amy two years later, benefited greatly from my care as our father was working two and one-half jobs simultaneously and had little time for anything else. And it was a win for me. I truly enjoyed doing it. It was not work. We had ten great years together.

I never saw my baby sister again as I was drafted into the Army during the Vietnam era. After basic training in New Jersey I was sent overseas to a non-combat zone at the forward edge of the Cold War battle area in Europe for the duration.

When I returned to America and subsequently released honorably from the service, I met my big girl sister, Amy, now on Cape Cod. I watched her mature and endure her teenage years from a distance. I only saw her at family gatherings. She didn't need me anymore and gravitated more towards my wife and our daughter when we were together. Amy's three brothers formed our own click, separate but equal from the girls, at holidays and vacation times.

When last I saw my teenage sister, Amy, she was off to college and I was off to the rest of my own life back down south of the Mason-Dixon Line.

I met my third sister Amy when she returned home to join the family business in West Dennis. I hardly recognized this woman who purported to be my sister. She had graduated from college and had taken her degree into the world of commerce for a few years. But now she was back.

During her collegiate time she had grown taller than I while retaining the cherubic beauty she'd been born with. Over the years following her return to the Cape I could see that the center of power in the family and its business was devolving off our parents and onto her. She married the boy next door and merged the family business with another.

We lost our Mom all too soon. Before she left she told us, the two older brothers, she was bequeathing the title of head of clan to our sister, Amy. Neither of us objected. Amy took our widower dad into her home and nurtured him for a dozen years. Her husband was a prince about it. He had always been a better son to our parents than any of us three brothers.

Amy left us six months before Dad passed away. Amy'd only lived half a life time. Dad likely died of a broken heart. Our father was laid to rest between the remains of his loving wife and loving daughter, the two women who cherished him and who he cherished until his last breath.

I do not mourn my sisters Amy. I am still mad at them. As the eldest, I should've gone first. They should've had to bury me, not I them. I love you, Amy.

Bob Surrette

Sister's Friend

I am no sister,
but I am a sister's friend;
I understand what
it is to be related;
I know what it is
to be committed to someone,
and I am not concerned
in the least
that blood does not flow
between us;
I am also not concerned
with the politics
of relationship,
for we are infinitely
matched up
on an emotional map
we don't need directions
to read,
and we know how to find
our way through it
to the very end
of the road.

Linda Holbrook

Two Sisters Speak

Seven generations forward,
Seven generations back occurred yesterday
The day the century plant bloomed.
Deep crevices in the earth rearranged themselves.
The day two sisters said I love you,
I forgive you
Wiping the slate clear
Not looking back on the days
We stopped each other's heart
With our attitudes, with karma.

She said, "I love you" and I said, "what did you say?"
She said, "Let's start from a clean slate."
She said," Please forgive me for all the times
I slighted you or hurt you."
She reeled off so many things
I couldn't take it all in.

She said we are almost twins.
I said we are blood.
I've always known you as sister, as blood.
We're nearing 79 years
on this planet together.
Closer to laughter
Looking into each other's brown eyes.
A deeply tucked away prayer
For connection.

Every word flowed
The moment we talked.
Each voice neutral
As in deciding where to eat.
In ordinary time
Like none before.

Something bloomed yesterday
And I'm attending.

Ann Griffin

Crisis in Syria

Rainy morning hailing a cab
my driver tells me he is Syrian
asks permission to play music
chanting calls me,
listen, he says, it is from the Koran
it is called the heart of God

How many innocent sisters
have died in Syria

I listen
a cocoon away from rain
or blare of horns
find myself praying

How many sisters have died in Syria
as innocents succumb

We arrive
he opens the door for me
stands upright
I shake his hand

How many innocent sisters have died

Barbara Truncellito

Requiem for Cynthia

A dozen painted ponies
Will gallop over your grave
I want you to lie down here, he said
Even when it rains
The lightning bolts will fool you
But the life will not return
Not green or verdant pasture
Can cool the ardent pain
As the loss succumbs to glory,
And glory turns to fame
Your name it will endure, he said
You will pass this way again
Your body won't be the same, he said
And there will be no pain
So smear the dusty ashes
On the forehead of your faith
The church bells ringing out
To the believers scattered here
They have come in vain to mourn for you
They cannot see my dear,
That you are no longer here…

Christine Price

My Sisters Are Many

My sisters are many—
Some blood, some not;
Some faces are clear,
Some, not a lot.

Though years sometimes fade
A face or a name,
My life without each
Would not be the same.

One of my sisters,
Although twice my age—
Life without her
I could not even gauge.

Another sister,
Not blood, but a friend—
After a loss,
Helped my heart mend.

I can close my eyes
And yet I can see
How each of my "sisters"
Made me . . . Me.

Barbara Vetter

I can't imagine what it will feel like if my sister dies.
I've known her since I was three. She's never not been there.

Would she want to continue this way?
How can I know. She's sedated.

I can't ask her: "Kath, what do you want to do?"

Sitting here, surrounding her in Light,
I wait to see if she can rally.

Jyoti Wind

Sisterhoods

Sisterhoods
Are bound by blood
Are bound by friendship
Are bound to God

Sisterhoods
Express feelings
Employ expression
Encompass the world

Sisterhoods
Unify the feminine
Unify yin to yang
Uphold life
...in a myriad of ways.

Holly Hunter

Can You Draw Me?

My sister Shirley answered the Can You Draw Me ad in the newspaper and won a scholarship to Abbott Art School in Washington, D.C. As soon as she graduated, she married her art teacher and they had a daughter. Her husband didn't want any responsibility. He hid bills under the couch and threw the baby across the room. Fortunately the baby landed on the couch.

Shirley's husband was a World War II veteran who kept a loaded German Luger in the house. One evening, when Shirley was preparing dinner, she felt like stabbing him with the butcher knife. Afraid of her potential violence adding to his, she took the baby and left him. She quit art school and became a successful commercial artist.

I didn't answer that ad. At the Corcoran School of Art, I took one course in commercial art and hated it. Drawing grocery, furniture and appliance ads was of no interest to me. The only assignments to my liking were textile and clothing designs, where I could be creative by using my painting skills on designs related to my interest in fabrics.

Many years later, when I lived in Stinson Beach, Elizabeth Penniman, a curator, asked me to be in a self-portrait exhibition sponsored by the Bolinas Museum. The idea of looking at my face in the mirror every day for an extended period of time wasn't appealing. I preferred younger models. My first thought was to show the pastel portrait I did on my fiftieth birthday.

But that was too depressing. I thought about doing an assemblage of personal objects. That would be more symbolic, more abstract and therefore more interesting. Then I remembered that I had a new blank book.

▶

For the next two months I recorded my thoughts and sketches for a self-portrait in that square blue book. It became a daily journal. On April 23, 1993, I wrote, "Cesar Chavez died today. The sky cried. They had a mass and sang songs for him." I wondered, when I am gone, will anyone sing songs for me? My husband, Harold commented on one of the sketches, "You look like some artist ready to take a flying leap into the rolling donut hole – or something."

I sketched my face in sorrow and stillness, as my mother, as my grandmother. I covered my face with grease paint and made ten face prints. They attracted gnats, ants and self- descriptive words: left-handed, blind visionary, old child, wounded healer, dream dancer.

I love motion and resist fixing moments in time. I don't like to have my photograph taken or my voice recorded. In my drawings, an open network of lines records a series of moments by layering paths of motion. Much of my art has to do with motion. People say an artist's work is self-reflective. If we are each the model, why even hire another person to pose? Is it to avoid looking in the mirror? Can I draw me?

Claudia Chapline
First published in catalog, Self Portraits: True Stories,
Bolinas Museum, Bolinas, CA 1993

now
I am remembering
when we first met
your palm on my shoulder
the way my head turned
in slow motion
my chin leading the way
my eyes following close behind
to gaze into the face of an angel
your long strawberry blonde hair
curtaining your emerald green eyes
the gentle smooth curve
of your forehead
the sweep of your nose
especially the gift of your smile
truly love at first sight
and despite our human foibles
always love
I feel you with me now
24 years after you really sprouted wings and flew on
but
oh the longing for your laughter
longing for our tears
sharing our hopes and fears
I still see your face
and the look in your eyes
silk screened on my heart
oh glorious
epiphany of light that you are
Tajalli*

*Tajalli - a Sufi name meaning: The Epiphany of Light, or the
crowning glory of light

Dakini Lynn Marlowe

The Search for Steph

Much of my life has been shrouded in a strange mystery that became something of a great obsession for me. Perhaps it was that my desire for a sister was so great, but I started to become convinced that I had a sister already. From the time I was a child, when I was in public I would search the faces of those around me looking for a glimmer of recognition. Where was my sister?

I puzzled greatly over this. My parents wouldn't have given a child away. My mother was such a goody-two-shoes that she wouldn't have had a baby before my dad came along. Oh, this just didn't make sense. Still I searched – hopefully or hopelessly. I didn't know which.

Years passed and even though I tried to forget my obsession, it remained. I read an article about lost fetuses being absorbed into their twins and the memory remaining with the living twin. I tried to placate myself with this idea, but it just didn't quite fit.

Then, one cold winter day, my mother made a shocking confession. She spoke in a flat, emotionally dead voice as she struggled to get the truth out. It was the story of how she had been raped in her early twenties and became pregnant. It interrupted her college studies as she was sent to a home for unwed mothers. There she was routinely shamed for her condition. After the appropriate amount of time she bore a baby girl she named Stephanie Scott Dawson. Against all advice she had insisted on seeing the baby she was about to give away. After about two weeks Stephanie was in the hands of her new adoptive parents and Mom went back to her life, finished college and went on to marry my father. She had buried the memory as far into the depths of her consciousness as she could, and had only recently recovered it.

The truth was that there was a sister out there who shared my blood. She was a real person, not just a piece of my imagination run wild. How did I know for all those years that Stephanie existed? I'm thinking shared cell memory, but your guess is as good as mine.

The search for Steph goes on, but now I know I am not just dropping my marbles all over the place. Somewhere there is a sister – and she's mine.

Laurie Kay Olson

Sister Talk

We were waiting for the school bus, my sisters and brother and I, six of us in grade school, with only the youngest one still at home. Rhoda must have been in kindergarten. Like the rest of us girls, she wore a cotton dress and her only pair of shoes. Between the hem of her dress and the top of her bobby socks I noticed numerous dark smudges.

"Rhoda," I said in a big sister voice, "Go wash your legs before the bus comes."

"Those are not dirt," she said. "They're bruises." Her voice begged for understanding.

"Bruises?"

"I've been learning to ride the bike."

"Oh. Okay, then."

So many bruises, so many falls, but when Rhoda decided to learn a skill, she was determined. In short order she mastered the bike. The bruises faded.

Rhoda was born when I was six. Engaged in our own journeys and mostly living apart since childhood, we have skipped in and out of each other's explorations with resources, encouragement, and shared memories. Two among seven siblings, we are both middles. Three girls, a boy, and three more girls. I'm the middle one of "the big girls" and Rhoda is the middle one of "the little girls." I recall watching her crawl across the living-room floor, dark red curls bouncing. Of course she has no such memory of me. When she started paying attention, I seemed almost grown.

▶

Dad needed a crew. He made do with girls and never seemed to favor his son. We fed chickens and gathered eggs. We held sheep for shearing, we tromped the hay Dad forked onto the pickup, and we gently set baby chicks under brooders while Dad spread mash on newspapers and filled gallon watering jugs, capping each with the wide lid that was the watering tray and tipping them over in one quick motion, spilling little. When the baby chicks drank, bubbles of air would go into the jug and more water would come into the tray.

In the house we helped Mom with cleaning, laundry, and meals, learning such skills as how to guide a knife between the joints of a skinned pullet for frying, how to set the tables for nine.

In her turn Rhoda learned to say the little ditty that made sure nothing was omitted: bread and butter, salt and pepper, knives, forks, spoons, plates, and tumblers. We put out a pitcher of milk, raw like the butter, from our own cows. We learned how to bake cakes and tollhouse cookies.

Among us we learned piano, violin, clarinet, trumpet, flute, and trombone. We'd get out the Golden Song book and off we'd go. Driving anywhere in the car, Mom and Dad sang duets. Soon we kids were singing harmonies.

Because of our age difference, I don't have a lot of memories of doing things with Rhoda except when the whole family went together. Most years in September we camped at Mt. Katahdin and climbed to Baxter Peak, the highest point in Maine. Being little could be an advantage on the trail. Rhoda went up those boulders like a goat. If Mom missed Rhoda she knew she was up ahead and would soon show herself. The pleasure of hiking together, the size of those granite boulders, the cool mineral taste of Chimney Pond water stayed with us.

▶

That's a lot to have in common—even before you look at personality. We were the philosophers of the family, the ones most likely to raise our heads above what was all around us and ask how it got to be that way and what we should understand about life.

One of the resources Rhoda brought into the family was the Myers-Briggs Type Indicator, or MBTI. She sent us the "tests" (there are no wrong answers, only choices) and gave us our scores at a family workshop, Mom and Dad, all seven of us, our spouses and children. We learned to see one another with a fresh awareness. Dad, Mom, Winky, Wayne, and Brenda all scored high on the skills that keep our institutions going, quietly providing social continuity and guarding against changes that are too sudden or too sweeping. With these five around, you were never going to throw out the baby with the bathwater. Even Merry, a nurse, was an institution person, though subjectively so where the other five were persons of objective principal. Only Debbie, the youngest, and Rhoda and I, cared little for protocol. An action person, Deb learned to fly a small plane.

Rhoda and I were both inquisitive, but where she was a bit of a scientist and willing to take a leap into connection with spirit, I was a relationship person, valuing friendships and family. I wanted to know why people weren't getting along on this planet and what we must do to get into harmony. I was willing to throw out the whole culture and start over, if that's what it took, though I had to get out of the house to do it. Rhoda understood my lack of allegiance to Yankee cultural assumptions. I was lucky to have her, because, of course, the protocol-minded people in our family, all six of them, thought I was nuts. They didn't get me.

Rhoda did. With us it was the talking that mattered, the many conversations about what was going on, who was really controlling our country, the health value of being cheerful. The talks would vary, depending on who was gathered round the table. When Merry or Deb was present we did not criticize the church

▶

of our childhood. Merry needed only "that old time religion," and Deb needed a comfortable faith she didn't have to puzzle out. We learned not to talk spirituality with Wayne, who had made a religion out of science. Winky and Brenda were easy to include, often enjoying talk beyond their usual interests. For Rhoda and me, the obvious silliness of our childhood religion didn't mean there was nothing beyond the material world. We loved to talk about our experiences of spirit and soul-growth. We freed ourselves into an ever amazing awareness and became confident women. This essay is packed with love for her, for her courage and acute intelligence.

We have been glad to have each other to talk to. At times we were almost aliens in the thick of such a determined practicality and acceptance of the world as it was that our willingness to imagine other worlds was either unwelcome or too weird to puzzle out. We were the only ones who spoke the language of possibility, who saw the unseen.

And then there was the sheer beauty of life. I remember an evening some years ago when Wayne and Rhoda took out guitars and sang a duet they had been practicing. Their gentle strumming, their sweet voices winding together in harmony, took my breath away.

Although several of us live outside of Maine, we still gather there. We have plans for this fall. Perhaps all of us will make it "home' this year.

Patricia Lapidus

Dreaming Through

You dreamed the dream
and dared to find the way
to pull me through
the dark woods,
and now I am enjoying
the light you pulled me into,
but you were the light,
sister-friend,
as you have been
for many years -
no one is more dear to me
and as we face age's
problems and challenges
I want you to know
that if need be
I will come to pull you
through the darkness,
although I have to wonder how
any darkness could find you,
since you walk in light
as bright as any star
in the sky.

Linda Holbrook

Oh Sister, My Sister

I feel like your wisdom is leaking into the ground
Like the morphine drip hospice has hooked you up to.
Just before your last breath
Leaves you a shell of who you were,
I hold your hand and call your angels to you,
Lest you leave here alone,
Arriving there with no one waiting for you.
Oh sister, my sister,
For 66 years we played the roles,
Me the oldest, initial greeter and now releaser,
You the younger, willing and faithful friend,
Like the games we played as children.
We danced around out differences,
Each firmly ensconced in attitudes not to be budged.
But underlying, love drifted in and out
Like snow on the beach in December.
And it's almost December now.
I don't think Christmas will find you here this year.
I think it will find you running with your dogs, Gus and Aja,
Who went before you
So they could lick you all over
When you arrive.
Oh sister, my sister,
If I could call you back
And know you could make it, I would.
But I am not the larger hand
That guides all of this.
I'm a pawn in the game of life as well.
So I will celebrate your life,
Climb some Colorado peaks for you,
And send your ashes to rest in the sea
With our parents.
I will miss you terribly.

Jyoti Wind

Braided Lives

Our lives are braided like challah,
its sacred yeast redolent
with family traditions
handed down l'dor v'dor,
generation to generation.
She asks, froggie, what's up?
My hunger abates nourished
by love that birthed us both.
Once again we are Lesincoo and Shelala,
endearments echo in shared veins.
We polish the tarnished silver,
set the table with blue and gold porcelain,
raise Grandma Frieda's rose-colored glasses,
and dine on challah and honey.

Leslie B. Neustadt

Bios

Diane L. Akins, a retired psychotherapist and trainer, lives in Denver, Colorado. "Longing," one of her short stories, was published in the June 2010 issue (No. 3) of *eFiction Magazine.* In addition, her poetry has appeared in *WestWard Quarterly*, *Write On! Poetry Magazette, The Poet's Art,* and *Living with Loss Magazine*; and two of her essays were published in *Unraveling Mysteries: An Anthology on Women and Aging* and *The Creative Arc: An Anthology on Writing*, respectively.

Arlene Sandra Bice of Macon, North Carolina, has published several books in various genres. Her words also appear in Silkworm, Oasis Literary Journal, Unraveling Mysteries, The Creative Arc and is the delighted recipient of the Florence Poets Society Poet of Distinction Award.

Marie Carpenter began writing eight years ago with the Thursday Women's writing group. Marie loves her home and garden. Special interests are reading a good book, going on long walks, swimming in the early morning, taking the motor home out on long trips with her husband of 60 years.

Claudia Chapline, is a writer/artist living in Northern California. She is the author of six poetry books and two memoirs. She received a Lifetime Achievement Award from the Northern California Chapter of the Women's Caucus for Arts for her contributions to the arts in California.

Jane DeJonghe writes high country haiku from her cabin near Colorado's Mt. Evans Wilderness Area. Several of her haiku were included in the 2013 anthology, "Lifting the Sky, Southwestern Haiku and Haiga" by Dos Gatos Press. Contact her at: janedejonghe@yahoo.com

Charlene Ellington is a practitioner of the healing arts at her healing center, Energetic Transformations, animal communicator and writer.

Susan Fernie, when she was in her early 50's, discovered the joy of writing. The highlight of her week is when she gathers with others to read their work and to write together. This has enriched her life and expanded her exploration of the joy of putting words together into a coherent piece.

Carole Fults is originally from Michigan and has lived happily in upstate New York for the last twenty years. She recently had a piece accepted into the Berkshire Festival of Women Writer's Anthology and has been published in the International Expressive Arts Therapy Association magazine. You can find Carole on her blog at www.carolefults.com.

Priscilla Gifford, 86, is a retired nursing home social worker who moved to Boulder in 2002 from upstate New York for the balmy winters, and to be near her artist daughter and grandson. She and her daughter, Anne produced a children's book, "Spike the Dhog" in 2013.

Ann Griffin is a published poet. Her articles on end of life care have appeared in the magazine Transitions Unlimited. She has compiled a Memoir Video highlighting her life with painting, poetry, photography, T'ai Chi and gardening. She lives in Lafayette, CO

Marietta Harris is an accomplished musician and vocalist, writer. author and motivational speaker She is a native San Franciscan who has traveled the globe. You will be encouraged as you read how she changed her life and how she has broken through to "*The Other Side of Alzheimer's, a caregiver's story.*" She continues to speak about this disease to help family members survive She has always enjoyed good mysteries. "**The Gospel Choir Murder**" is her first.

▶

Elena Hoffrichter is a writer and artist, using words, pastels, and embroidery thread to create poems, paintings and needle art, expressing the beauty she sees in the world.

Linda Holbrook Poet, photographer, world traveler. Yeats International Summer School, Sligo, Ireland; Aspen Writers Conference, Aspen, Colorado; ESL Teachers Conference, Bratislava, Czech.; British Studies Certificate, CU Boulder BA Journalism, Univ. of Georgia MA Education/ESL Emphasis, CU Denver ; German Language Study, CU Boulder and Regensburg, Germany

Holly Hunter is an herbalist and nutrition counselor. She has published three herbal workbooks, magazine articles, and poems. Currently she is working on a novel.

Trish Lindsey Jaggers, an award-winning Kentucky poet, educator, amateur photographer, vintage/antique collector, as well as wife, mother, and grandmother, has published in numerous literary magazines, journals, books, and anthologies. She makes her home on a small farm in Chalybeate, Kentucky, where she divides her time amongst the quiet spaces nature so abundantly offers, family, collecting, and full-time teaching at Western Kentucky University.

Trish Lapidus has published a memoir of her life in a community of spiritual hippies, *Sweet Potato Suppers: A Yankee Woman Finds Salvation in a Hippie Village.* Her poems appear in literary magazines including *Green Hills Literary Lantern, Off the Coast*, and *Peregrine. Gideon's River,* a novel, about family. *Red Hen's Daughter's* isa book of poems out of a farm childhood. Coming out this year: *The Last Years of a Satellite Farm: New Fires from Community Embers.*

▶

Marcella J. Lively holds a masters degree in Psychology and Counseling. She is the author of Peaceful Pregnancy Peaceful World and also of the musical, The Goddess Is Back In Style!

Dakini Lynn Marlow is a writer, artist, and healer living in Boulder, CO. She shares her gift of healing touch that she has gleaned throughout her life, studies, and practices at Sophia Sanctuary. Her brand new book of poetry and photos: Now: Poems For This Moment is now available. You may be "In Touch" with her at: lynnmarlow@comcast.net or visit the Sophia Sanctuary Facebook page.

Barbara McDaniel is a mystic, artist, writer, and Craniosacral Therapist living in Boulder, CO. She is a fresh empty-nester and recently fell in love. She is currently working on a book about perception and beauty.

Curtine Metcalf is a poet and free-lance writer, of mostly human-interest non-fiction. She has written for several regional publications and is proud to be a contributing author to four other published books. A passionate volunteer, animal and child activist, she strives to be a humanitarian, and believes real stories should be shared.

Cindy Morris, msw is an author, astrologer, presenter, and collaborator with crystologist and intuitive healer John Corsa in bringing more LOVE to Earth and her inhabitants. http://IgniteYourSoulPotential.com

Jo-Ann Jeannine Kling Murdach was born in Glenwood, Minnesota, and currently lives in Hayward, Ca. with her husband of 48 years. They have 2 sons, 3 grandchildren, and many nieces and nephews and their children.

Leslie B. Neustadt is a retired Assistant Attorney General of the state of New York and the author of *Bearing Fruit: A Poetic Journey* (2014, Spirit Wind Books). Her writing is illuminated by her Jewish upbringing and expresses her experiences as a woman, daughter, wife, mother, cancer patient and incest survivor. www.LeslieNeustadt.com.

Laurie Kay Olson, writes poetry, short fiction, articles, and essays, and is currently working on a book of humorous narratives. During the 1990s she worked for the *Colorado Daily* newspaper as a journalist and a humor columnist. Currently she writes articles for PetsLady.com and InventorSpot.com.

Julie Ann Orecchio is the third generation to reside in Colorado. Her age is 74, and she enjoys writing. She wrote a poem about the American flag, and was proud to say it was published. Julie belongs to a women's writing group who meets once a month to critique others' pieces.

Annette Price is a storyteller, a business woman, a folkloric herbalist, and a lover of horses. She graduated as an EGCM coach in 2011and founded On The Wings of a Horse coaching practice. Annette Price @ Dragonfly Farm, Certified Equine Gestalt Coach www.onthewingsofahorse.com www.healinghorseregistryinternational.com

Christine Price was born and raised in South Africa and currently calls Lake Gaston, VA "home"....for now! She has a double Master's Degree in Education and is a graduate of the Devon Homeopathy School in the UK. She is married and has two children.

Terra Rafael has supported women's health as a midwife, then as an Ayurveda practitioner since 1981. She is enjoying her life with family and friends in Colorado.

▶

Rene Ratchek is a student of life, homeopathy and herself.

Prema Rose has worn many hats through this journey of her life including Broadway Actress, Midwife, Filmmaker, Healer, Teacher, Writer, Mother, and Grandmother. Each adventure has enlivened and rooted her in her ultimate passion for Spiritual awakening. www.mccsproducions.com

Bev Simpson is a Denver native, and mother of three children. She enjoys spending time with them and her six grown grandchildren whenever possible. Her hobbies include writing, painting and crafts. She loves meeting people and enjoys the Writers' Group that she has belonged to for over eight years.

Nancy Schluntz, interfaith minister, is an intuitive animal communicator, animal Reiki practitioner, and pet loss bereavement counselor. Formerly executive director of a mid-sized nonprofit agency, Nancy now volunteers as an animal caretaker at a nature center. She is an author, public speaker, grandmother, and publishes a blog on her website, www.NancySchluntz.com. Her book, *Hand in Paw, a Journey of Trust and Discovery*, is available on Amazon.com.

Karen Stewart has personally dealt with addiction and many challenges in her child and adult life. In 1994 she obtained her Master's degree in Social Work, and has over 25 years working in the fields of mental health, HIV/AIDS and addiction. Ten of those years have been working with Doctors Without Borders throughout Asia and Africa as a Mental Health Officer and Coach.

April Bennett Stone is the mother of two children and a German Shepherd, one of four sisters and a recovering lawyer.

Bob Surrette lives, laughs, loves and writes on Cape Cod with his wife of 44 years. He has three grandchildren, one of whom resembles his three sisters.

▶

Lesley Tabor is a life-long writer and seeker of personal and cultural healing, and a grandmother. She's currently in retreat, after a couple of years of involvement with Occupy Albany. She has published poems and essays in several anthologies, self-published two poetry chapbooks, and has written (but not published) three novels.

Barbara Truncellito is a published poet. She ran her own Press called Fragile Twilight Press for twenty years. She's been published by the Cole Foundation for the Arts in Baker's Dozen Vol. III She lives in NYC and on Long Beach Island, N.J.

Bobbie Vetter is 82 years of age, and although a Colorado resident for the past 48 years, she was born in Brooklyn, NY. After years of secretarial work, Bobbie owned (and groomed in) a pet grooming shop for 15 years. She's been writing—poetry and prose—for as far back as she can remember and has been published in Westward Quarterly, Anthology on Writing, Anthology on Women and Aging, Prairie Times, Living With Loss, and belongs to a Women's Writers Group.

Jyoti Wind is a poet and author. Her poetry and prose has recently been published at elephant journal online, Rising Sun Magazine and Crone Magazine. She has self-published several books of poetry and prose, a childhood memoir, and four anthologies. Jyoti also leads women's weekly writing groups. She is a mother, grandmother, great grandmother and a walker.

Artist's Bio
Kathleen Spencer Johns is an award winning painter. In her paintings Kathleen expresses the intimacy of life through conveying the depths of her emotional connections with her subject. Kathleen was born in Schenectady, New York, the fourth of ten children. Kathleen has lived in Boulder, Colorado for the last thirty years and has two grown sons. Kathleen is the fine arts teacher at Shining Mountain Waldorf High School in Boulder. www.kathleenspencerjohns.com

Special Thanks:

To Arlene, Cindy and Jennie for their beautiful hearts.
To Barb and her being there.
To Prema for her timely presence.
To Lanai for his heart and expertise.
To Kathleen for her generosity of spirit.
To all the women in the writing groups
and to everyone who contributed!!!!